My Life After Trauma Handbook

by the same authors

My Anxiety Handbook
Getting Back on Track
Sue Knowles, Bridie Gallagher and Phoebe McEwen
Illustrated by Emmeline Pidgen
ISBN 978 1 78592 440 8
eISBN 978 1 78450 813 5
Part of the Handbook Series

My Intense Emotions Handbook
Manage Your Emotions and Connect Better with Others
Sue Knowles, Bridie Gallagher and Hannah Bromley
Illustrated by Emmeline Pidgen
ISBN 978 1 78775 382 2
eISBN 978 1 78775 383 9
Part of the Handbook Series

The Anxiety Survival Guide
Getting through the Challenging Stuff
Bridie Gallagher, Sue Knowles and Phoebe McEwen
Illustrated by Emmeline Pidgen
ISBN 978 1 78592 641 9
eISBN 978 1 78592 642 6

of related interest

Trauma is Really Strange
Steve Haines
Illustrated by Sophie Standing
ISBN 978 1 84819 293 5
eISBN 978 0 85701 240 1
Part of the '... is really strange' Series

The Strange and Curious Guide to Trauma
Sally Donovan
Illustrated by Emmi Smid
ISBN 978 1 78775 747 9
eISBN 978 1 78775 748 6

MY LIFE AFTER TRAUMA HANDBOOK

Surviving and Thriving using Psychological Approaches

Bridie Gallagher, Sue Knowles,
Reggie Worthington and Jade Baron
Illustrated by Chloe Collett

Jessica Kingsley Publishers
London and Philadelphia

First published in Great Britain in 2023 by Jessica Kingsley Publishers
An imprint of Hodder & Stoughton Ltd
An Hachette Company

1

A CIP catalogue record for this title is available from the British Library and the Library of Congress

ISBN 978 1 83997 128 0
eISBN 978 1 83997 129 7

Printed and bound in Great Britain by Clays Ltd

Jessica Kingsley Publishers' policy is to use papers that are natural, renewable and recyclable
products and made from wood grown in sustainable forests. The logging and manufacturing
processes are expected to conform to the environmental regulations of the country of origin.

Jessica Kingsley Publishers
Carmelite House
50 Victoria Embankment
London EC4Y 0DZ

www.jkp.com

Contents

Acknowledgements

Our biggest thank you goes to all the young people who have contributed to this book, through their comments, suggestions, reflections, ideas and quotes. For all the young people who have taught us so much about the after effects of trauma, their courage and wish to help themselves and others, we feel honoured that you've been able to share your experiences with us.

Bridie would like to thank her endlessly present and patient friends and family for staying connected and available through all the ups and downs – you know who you are. She is grateful for so many supportive colleagues who, despite working in beyond unreasonable conditions, have taught her so much about patience (not something she was born with) and tenacity. Bridie's biggest thanks go to her children Anna and Reuben, who have made her a much better psychologist with their 'direct' feedback about her own coping and emotional responses. They make her laugh out loud every single day and for that she is truly grateful.

Sue would like to thank her husband Ben, whose support and belief in her has been unwavering, and her son Tom who begrudgingly agreed to read through the book and comment (*still* for ice cream). Warmest thanks to Pam for supporting Sue through her own trauma journey, and for being her fairy godmother when she's needed it. She would also like to dedicate this book to her dad; although he never really understood what she did for a career, he was always proud. Finally, she would like to give big thanks, both personally and professionally, to her team at Child and Family Services at Changing Minds (CMCAFS), for their ongoing enthusiasm and support.

Reggie would like to give huge thanks to his mum and dad, for believing in him and being there no matter what; his Nana and Grandad Lolly for their unconditional love and generosity; his Aunty Clare, Uncle Mark, Uncle John and Aunty Jane for encouraging him to follow his dreams. Thanks to Sedbergh School, in particular Mr Newman, Mr Bunday, Dr Hoskins, Mr Davies and Mr Seymour, for setting him on the right path and helping him be the best that he can be.

Jade would like to thank the whole team who have worked so hard to put together this book.

A big thank you to our very thorough draft readers, Gill and Steve, for their insightful comments and reflections. Thank you to Gill for sharing her knowledge and supporting with practical queries, but also for reflective conversations that helped to shape the book.

Members of the Blackburn with Darwen Voice Group for Children in Our Care were so welcoming and shared their thoughts and experiences, and for this we are so grateful (and the snacks and brews).

Biggest thanks to Beth, CJ, Jake, James, Lauren, Lola, Kim, Rach and all the young people – and young-ish people – who shared their views and stories within this book.

A massive thanks to Terry Angus for kindly agreeing to spend some time with us, thinking through how physical activity can support people to feel more in control of their trauma reactions, but also, most importantly, the need to understand context and accessibility.

Our warmest thanks to Suzi Wrenshaw from Trauma Therapy Manchester for providing consultation to us around the use of movement and yoga within trauma therapy, sharing ideas and her wealth of knowledge, and for spending the best part of a rainy Saturday with us.

Finally, to our team at Jessica Kingsley Publishers, particularly Amy, who has been with us from the start. Thank you for your belief in us, and our projects, and your drive to make therapy and resources accessible for all young people.

Preface: What Just Happened?

Adversity is part of life and we all have experiences that we've found difficult and distressing or where we've felt really scared and alone. We wanted to write this book because as psychologists we see the impact of trauma every single day in our work with young people, families and the teams of people that support them. We wanted to acknowledge and write about the huge impact of both the everyday trauma that often goes ignored and not talked about, when families are in situations that mean they sadly aren't able to provide the safety and care that children need enough of to survive and thrive, and those traumas that make the news and shock people to their core. We've tried to think about and support recovery from both, which was tough. It also means we cover a lot of different ways of understanding and managing traumatic responses.

We don't expect you to sit and read this whole book as though it is a tour guide that can take you smoothly on a journey of recovery. We rather wanted it to be a source of ideas and stories that you can dip in and out of, take the bits that feel useful and leave the bits you don't. We imagine you will come back to it as you try things out and learn more about yourself and how you are responding to whatever event or experiences brought you to pick it up. We want the voices of all the people who were brave enough to share their own stories to keep you company and remind you that not only are you not alone, but nothing stays the same and there's always hope.

When we set out to write this book, we knew it would be stressful and we knew it might bring up some difficult thoughts, feelings and memories for us all. We didn't know that there would be a global pandemic and that life would change for us and everyone around us in ways that we couldn't ever imagine. We're not sure what sort of book it would have been if we had written it before the pandemic...but we guess it would have been different because we were unable to see each other much, or meet up in person for long periods of time, or talk about our ideas and reflections as often. The people who contributed were often just voices over email rather than people we went to meet. The world suddenly seemed a scarier place but yet we spent more time with the people we love. It got harder to think straight. We know this is what happens when we are scared and under stress, but this was a very real reminder.

It's likely that reading this book will be tough for many of you, either all the way through or just in parts, and we wanted to share that at times it was tough writing it. But it was also wonderful and kept us working together and pulling each other through because we know that if we can share information, ideas and strategies that make a positive difference to any young people or connect with them when they are feeling scared and alone, then it will have been more than worth it.

When it gets tough, we urge you to do what we did – take a break, make a cup of tea/hot chocolate, be kind to yourself and reach out to the people who make you feel safe and okay.

Bridie and Sue xx

◇ Chapter 1 ◇

What's Trauma?

A traumatic experience is one where there is significant harm, or risk of harm, to yourself or someone else. You might experience the event yourself or might witness it happening to someone close by, or you may even be affected by hearing about a traumatic event that someone close to you has been through.

Most people will go through a difficult, or traumatic, experience in their lives. In fact, lots of people will go through more than one. Often, we'll be able to get through these events with the help of other people, heal and even grow and learn from them. Sometimes, though, these traumatic events will have a really big impact on us, and we'll experience trauma reactions that continue to affect us for months or even years to come. This book focuses on the after effects of trauma – the way that it can affect our brains and bodies, our emotional responses and behaviours, the way that we see the world, and our relationships – and considers how to get through or cope with trauma reactions, and even grow and thrive in our lives after the traumatic experience/s.

There are two main types of trauma that we'll think through in this book: post-traumatic stress and developmental/complex trauma.

What are trauma reactions?

Post-traumatic stress describes the understandable, intense psychological and bodily reactions that someone can have after a traumatic event. In this book, we'll spend some time exploring different reactions, getting an understanding of them, and thinking about how to cope with or feel more in control of them.

We know that some people can see something terrible happen, or even have a traumatic thing happen to them (like an accident or a crime being committed), and then very quickly go back to their everyday lives without feeling that things have changed much. But for many people, there's a period of acute stress that follows a traumatic experience while their brain tries to make sense of what happened, and their body tries to keep them safe and make sure nothing else bad happens to them. This is totally normal. Acute means sudden and intense at first, but then it passes. But if this stress carries on for a number of months and is 'chronic' or 'longer term', this could interfere with your life a lot and might begin to meet the criteria for a 'disorder', which is a label given by a psychiatrist or psychologist. A 'disorder' is a short way of describing a set of symptoms someone is experiencing. In terms of trauma, a diagnosis of a 'disorder' doesn't mean that the person will always have these symptoms or meet the criteria for the disorder. It means that, at that time, it's helpful to recognize that they're experiencing significant symptoms that meet the criteria for a disorder.

The label or 'diagnosis' of post-traumatic stress disorder (PTSD) was first introduced in the mid-1980s. We have included a list of the criteria for PTSD in Appendix I, so you can see how a professional decides whether what's happening to you means it's helpful for you to have this label or not. There's a lot of jargon that we'll try and help you to understand in the rest of the chapter.

We'll talk through these traumatic reactions in more detail in the following chapters, and then think about some strategies that can help us to cope with, or get through, these. In addition to all these more negative 'symptoms', there are also some positive changes that people can discover when they've been through traumatic events. These positive changes occur when people have started to make sense of, and are working through, their traumatic experience. We cover these in more detail in Chapter 13 (Surviving to Thriving: Post-Traumatic Growth).

Lots of events can be defined as traumatic. Here are some of the main ones that young people might experience:

- Abuse – emotional, physical and sexual

- Bullying, and threatening or intimidating behaviour

- Robbery

- Being kidnapped or taken hostage

- Terrorist attack

- Natural disaster

- Car accident

- Fire

- Life-threatening illness.

It's often traumatic to see or hear any of these things happening to you or another person. When something really scary and unexpected happens, it's entirely normal for us to experience intense and overwhelming feelings like fear, helplessness or horror. Trauma can also be present if something not on this list but very upsetting happens, and at least for a short time, our 'internal resources' (our coping strategies and ways we keep ourselves feeling safe and present in the world) are completely overwhelmed.

Why are some people more affected than others by bad things that have happened?

Lots of things affect how we respond when bad things happen, including who we are. Some people are more likely to experience trauma, and some things make us more likely to have more responses or 'symptoms' that meet the criteria for a diagnosis:

- Our sex and gender identity.

- How old we are (and if something happens at an important time in our development when we should be focusing on other things).

- Race (which interacts with gender and other risk factors).

So, these sorts of things can interact to increase our risk of being exposed to a traumatic event and also impact the amount of support we might have. For example, being female *and* being an ethnic minority makes us more likely to be exposed to potentially traumatic experiences due to sexual/racial inequality, but this doesn't mean we're any less able to manage the impact, just that it's more likely to happen to us. Having an existing mental health problem, on the other hand, would make it more likely that we would experience symptoms of post-traumatic stress as well as making us more vulnerable to trauma (people with serious mental health problems are more likely to be the victim of a crime, for example).

Here are some other things that make you more likely to receive a diagnosis of PTSD:

- If you have less money – this is called your 'socioeconomic status'.

- If you have any psychological difficulties you might have had before, like low mood or anxiety.

- If there are lots of problems in your family like conflict, or practical problems like housing and chronic illness.

- If other bad things have happened to you before.

- If you're someone who's particularly sensitive to stress, which we call someone's 'hyperreactive nervous system'.

- If the person causing you harm is someone close to you (which can feel more complicated than if it was a stranger).

Do any of these fit with you?

Also, there are some types of trauma that we know have a greater risk of receiving a PTSD diagnosis:

- If someone hurts you on purpose.

- If you thought that you were going to die.

- If you were physically harmed.

- If you saw someone else lose their life, especially where the scene was distressing.

- If the trauma involved the loss of a friend or someone you love.

- If it came out of nowhere, you had no control, and it was not easy to predict.

- If you were sexually assaulted.

The possible impact of neurodiversity on trauma reactions

Those of you who have been identified as autistic, have sensory processing difficulties or have other neurodivergence (such as pre-natal alcohol-related neurological disorders) might find that some of the trauma reactions we discuss in the following chapters may affect you even more. For example, you might find that you feel really on edge, jumpy or are startled easily. It might take a 'smaller' trigger to make you feel overwhelmed, burned out or shut down. You might be more likely to experience difficulties with sleep. It might be that you struggle more to communicate how you are feeling, or what has happened, to people around you. You also might feel emotions like anxiety or anger more strongly or have difficulties with focus and concentration. Everyone is different, and experiences trauma reactions differently, so working out how trauma affects you personally is a good start. The same strategies and advice that we give throughout the book should still be help-ful, and some of them might even be more relevant to you.

Take a pause

Seeing big lists of reactions or 'symptoms' can be a bit overwhelm-ing. We hope that it can also be reassuring and help you to know that what you're going through is to be expected and you're not alone. It can also be pretty normal to experience some reactions after being through a traumatic event, as we'll find out in the next few chapters.

What do we know helps us to recover quicker after a trauma?

- How people around us react is so important. If we're well supported and those around us are able to listen, be under-standing and empathic, then accept how we think and feel rather than trying to 'fix' or make things better, we're more likely to feel supported and safe.

- If those around us can stay away from blaming – 'Why didn't you...?' – or stigmatizing – 'Oh no, what will everyone think?' – and instead show care and nurture in whatever way they can.

- If we can make sense of what happened to us with a narra-tive that fits with how we see the world; for example, 'Bad things happen sometimes, and although it was scary and horrible at the time, it wasn't my fault. I did my best, and I'm able to cope when bad things happen in the future.'

- If we were able to use our fight or flight response and get away.

- If after the event we're able to do something that helps us to feel more in control of what happened and prevent it from happening again in the future, for example getting a house alarm or sharing information in the community about road safety after seeing an accident happen.

Keeping connected

Good quality social support can buffer us from stress, because friendships provide emotional support, caregiving and create a sense of being connected to others. However, the experience of trauma can lead us to feel disconnected, emotionally numb, and as if no one understands what we're going through. These lonely feelings can lead us to stop talking to our friends and family, which is the very thing that could help us through our difficulties. This is why we also talk in some detail about this in Chapter 4 and think about how we can reconnect and create safety in our relationships.

You might be thinking, 'What I'm feeling isn't on that list', and that's okay too. Some of our reactions and responses after a traumatic event are complicated and can be hard to put into words as they're overwhelming feelings in our bodies or a 'sense' of things being different. Trauma can change the meaning that we give to our lives. Young people sometimes tell us that they feel 'empty', 'alone' and don't care about anyone or even themselves.

Some of the reactions and feelings can attract other diagnoses or labels because young people tell us that they feel low in mood and even hopelessness, overwhelming grief, anxiety, fear, as if they can't trust other people anymore, that they're totally unable to focus or concentrate, having panic attacks, or feeling totally numb.

One of the most difficult reactions can be if we're making sense of a trauma and come to the conclusion that it was somehow our fault and that we deserved this terrible thing that happened. This self-blame creates feelings of *shame*. When we feel shame, we want to hide. This means that when we most need to reach out to others and get support, we're likely to withdraw and avoid connection and warmth from others, maybe feeling that we don't deserve it or that they will realize we're bad if we let them in (see Chapter 10 for more information on shame and how to work through this difficult emotion).

Sometimes rather than feeling emotions, we might feel the trauma in our bodies and become preoccupied with pain or another physical symptom. Trauma is understood to be often 'held in the body', maybe as pain or tension. We might even start to hear, see or feel things that aren't there.

There are lots of different reactions and responses talked about here. Have you recognized any of these in yourself? Or are there any you haven't thought about as being related to the traumatic event, but now think they might be?

It might be that you're not recognizing your experiences or reactions in what you've read so far. If so, keep reading, and see whether what you've experienced might fit more with developmental trauma or 'complex PTSD'.

What is 'complex PTSD' or developmental trauma?

Complex PTSD has been talked about since the early 1990s. A new term was needed to help us understand what happens when people have repeated traumas over a long period of time. This might be because someone in or out of your house was abusing you, because you were exposed to repeated aggressive and abusive behaviour between adults (domestic abuse) or because the adults who should have been caring for you were unable to meet your needs enough of the time to keep you safe (neglect). When a little person is in a house where adults aren't able to meet their needs, this is life threatening, so their body and brain will respond just the same as some of the traumas listed earlier in this chapter. But, when the little person experiences lots of traumatic events, or ongoing trauma, this will impact on something called the 'threat response'. When the 'threat response' is switched on repeatedly, this can have big additional impacts on the brain and body.

As well as some of the reactions seen in PTSD (listed earlier), some young people feel they don't know who they are (confusion about their identity) or find it hard to make decisions. They might find that other people seem hard to read and understand and might find it hard to know how to be in relationships. This can include finding it difficult to understand 'social rules' about what's okay and what's not okay in relationships and friendships. Maybe it's a feeling that others just don't 'get' them. Often people say that they have really big reactions and overwhelming emotions, but they find it hard to explain them, or they feel unable to cope and don't know how to get back to feeling okay again (which is called 'emotional dysregulation').

It's really unfair that the people who've had the most difficult experiences early in their lives often also don't have people around them who can model and teach them good coping strategies, help them understand what's happening to them, and also help them feel okay again. If you do have someone (relative, teacher or coach) who can do all these things, then you have a much better chance of recovering and thriving following repeated early trauma.

If you don't have an adult to help you recognize, understand and manage the understandable horrible big feelings that come from not getting what you need and/or being abused/seeing abuse, then you've got to find your own ways to cope with the scary situations and the reactions that come with it. You can sometimes end up using quite extreme and/or risky behaviours to cope and try to make yourself feel a bit better. When distress is overwhelming and there's no one to help you to feel comforted and safe, some people can even hurt themselves, use drugs or alcohol, or get into abusive relationships in order to try to feel okay. The problem is that many of these understandable coping responses have lots of unintended consequences that can put you at risk of more trauma. These ways of coping can also make it harder to connect with others and get the support you need to move on from the trauma and not feel as if you're constantly under threat from other people or going to be rejected by them.

Adverse childhood experiences (ACEs)

ACES are not ace. ACEs are difficult experiences that we come across in lots of young people's lives. These include having parents who are separated, parents who drink too much, parents who have their own mental health problems or are in prison, not having somewhere safe to live, and not having needs met enough of the time. You may not think of yourself as someone who has experienced developmental trauma, but there is increasing research into and understanding about the impact of difficult early experiences on how we grow and how healthy (physically as well as mentally) we are. These ACEs build up to increase stress and they impact the way that our bodies respond and how we see the world. It doesn't mean that we've had a terrible childhood and parents are often not to blame for these experiences; they're just doing their best in difficult situations. It can be important to remember this and consider some of the ACEs when we're thinking about the story that we tell ourselves to understand what led us to be coping with trauma reactions, what we're doing to cope, and when we think about what we need to do to feel safe and okay again.

Holding on to hope

It's so important to remember that for thousands and thousands of years humans have survived and even thrived in the face and aftermath of trauma. We're programmed to survive adversity. We also now know more about what helps us to recover from trauma and how to help people move on when they feel 'stuck' with trauma reactions.

Trauma therapy focuses on the re-processing or resolution of trauma memories. But this isn't what everyone needs to recover. You may not feel ready for this or might not feel that you need to do this to feel okay again. Most people who experience trauma don't receive therapy or have another opportunity to 'work through' and process memories of trauma, but they're mostly doing okay. This is why we wanted to write this book to help people find some safety without necessarily needing a therapist.

This book will help you to:

– understand your trauma reactions and how your brain and body are trying to keep you safe

– create safety to help your brain and body know that you survived, and the trauma is over

– create stability through routines, good self-care and positive activities

– find ways to manage the big feelings, bodily sensations and trauma reactions (nightmares and things called 'flashbacks' and 'dissociation') that can follow a traumatic event so that you can either tolerate them or find ways to feel okay in your body again

– make sense of what has happened to you through your story

– work through any feelings of shame or self-blame.

At this point, it's important to acknowledge that you may be reading this while still being bullied, abused, neglected or witnessing violence at home. If this is the case, we urge you to tell an adult what's happening so they can help you find safety and support. You need to be safe in order to work on the trauma reactions. There are some helplines and other ideas in Chapter 5.

How do we make sense of what happened? It was senseless!

It's not about working out why the trauma happened – sometimes we're not able to do this – but it's about understanding ourselves better and being able to find peace with how we might have had to cope or the impact that it's had on us and those around us. To do this we need to tell our story, even if it's just to ourselves.

Formulation

Often, as young people talk about the trauma they've experienced, it's not just what happened that they're struggling to live with, but how they understand what it means about themselves, other people and the world. For example, children nearly always blame themselves if their parents hurt them or can't care for them. This leads them to develop beliefs that can have a huge impact on how they feel and what they do: 'I'm not worth love and care', 'Other people aren't trustworthy', 'The world is uncaring and unpredictable'. This self-blame often leads to shame, and the shame leads them to hide and find ways to cope that don't involve opening up to others or being vulnerable.

What happened to us when we were little, and how we've coped when bad things have happened before, helps us to understand how we're coping with our feelings and reactions right now. These things from the past can be key to understanding how we feel about, react and respond to what's happening in our life right now.

But I don't want to think that deeply about things. Is this book still for me?

It's okay if you're not ready to talk about what happened and get into the meaning. It can still be useful to think about what effects the trauma has had on your life and how things might have changed for better or worse.

When talking about this in therapy with people who aren't ready to name their trauma experiences, Sue has sometimes thought with them about what they could refer to it as. Some people have chosen descriptions such as 'the bad thing' or 'when it was cloudy'. They have then been able to talk about how 'the bad thing' affected their lives and their views of themselves and others in a way that felt safer to them.

Because the book focuses on safety, stability and finding ways to cope with trauma reactions, you can just ignore the bits about formulation and meaning making until you feel ready, or for many people, these other three things are enough to feel ready to move on with their lives.

Chapter 2

How Does Trauma Affect Your Body/Brain?

When we've been through traumatic experiences, this can leave an imprint in our brain and impact on how we view the world and everyday situations. In this chapter, we're going to explore some of the common ways in which traumatic experiences can affect our brain and body, with some personal experiences from young people too. If you experience any of these reactions, we'll talk about ways to cope with these and feel more in control of your body and mind later on in the book.

What happens in our brain and body when we experience trauma?

Our body has an in-built survival ('threat') system, which means that we're hardwired to respond to potential threats in our environment. Above anything else, our brain and body prioritize our survival. To ensure that we've the best chance of surviving any potential threat, we've a specific area of our brain (our brainstem and amygdala) which works to make sure that we have the best chance of survival. However, these systems initially work in isolation from the rest of the brain, which means that they make a split-second decision on how to react to the threat, without using the thinking part of our brain. If we sense danger, we act before thinking. Basically, our threat system chooses the best option/reaction to keep us safe, without us even really knowing that this is happening.

Acting without thinking? Sounds dangerous!

Actually, thinking would be really unhelpful at this point...

'Oh look, there's a tiger! I wonder whether it's just eaten or if it's quite hungry...'

Too late! You've already been pounced on. Cleverly, our threat system just picks from a few survival strategies:

Option 1: Flight. Well, typically, our best chance of surviving is when we can run away from the threat so that we don't have to interact with it at all (which is known as our 'flight response') and can get out of there as quickly as we can.

Option 2: Fight. If we can't get away from the threat quickly enough, then it might be that by fighting or attacking it (i.e. our 'fight response'), we can scare it away, make it weaker, or prevent it from attempting to attack us in the future.

Option 3: Freeze. Our freeze response is when our body becomes tense and rigid but doesn't move. The survival hope from this one is that the threat will either not notice us, or will lose interest in us, and will then start to move away. Then, as our body is already tense and ready to move, we can either run away (our flight response) or catch the threat unawares (our fight response).

Option 4: Collapse/Shut down. If all other options aren't feasible, and the threat is still there and not likely to go away, then our body and mind try to help us to cope and get through the trauma in the best way that they can. At this stage, our body and mind start to shut down (to try to reduce any physical or emotional pain), and we might faint or collapse. Our mind may also disconnect from our body and we may dissociate (see section below).

What's really important to remember is that we don't choose which threat response we use. Our body makes a split-second decision based on the information that's available at the time as to which survival strategy is going to work best. Sometimes people feel shameful about not fighting back or running away, even though they didn't have a choice about the way their body reacted in the moment, when it was trying to help them survive what happened. We cover this a little more in Chapter 10.

Fight/flight/freeze responses in the body and brain

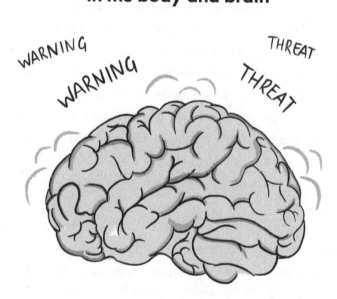

So, when we detect any type of threat in our environment, our brain quickly responds to make sure that we survive it. Imagine that it's late at night, and you're walking home from a friend's house. There's no one else around, and it's really dark outside. You suddenly hear footsteps behind you, quietly at first, but then they start to get quicker and louder as if someone's approaching behind you. Then you feel a hand grab your shoulder. What do you feel in that moment and what happens in your body? You might notice yourself gasp, or your breathing quicken. Your heart will probably start beating faster and might feel as if it's going to explode out of your chest. Your muscles will tense ready to react, you might get sweaty, and it's likely that your pupils will dilate (become wider). We call this the mobilization response, as your body is preparing itself to react to the threat. Your amygdala (the part of your brain which has detected the threat) triggers adrenaline to be released, which starts the body's survival response. This means that you're breathing quickly, and your air passages will have dilated, so that your muscles have the oxygen that they need to be prepared to react. Your blood vessels will also contract so that blood is pushed towards the parts of the body, such as the heart and lungs, that will be needed in a survival situation. When adrenaline has been released, the body also tends to feel less pain, which is why you might not feel pain at the time of the event but may notice bruises or cuts later. Adrenaline also releases glucose into the blood stream, which can lead to people feeling a 'super-human strength' and feeling more powerful and fast. People often report being 'hyper-aware' of their surroundings when their mobilization response has been triggered.

If you move into a freeze response, your muscles may become even more rigid (you would struggle to move them), you might feel a bit like a 'deer in headlights', frozen on the spot. You're likely to be breathing very quickly, which is called tachycardia. Your pupils may be very small or dilated, and your body is likely to be cold but sweaty. Sometimes when in this state, people find that they will even wet themselves (or worse) because they lose control of their bladder and/or bowels. When the threat moves away, then the person is able to run away or fight if needed.

So, your mobilization response has been triggered and your body is ready to react. What happens next? As described above, your body makes a split-second decision about what to do to maximize your chances of survival. So, when that hand goes on your shoulder, you might find yourself trying to run away or get out of the situation as quickly as you can (flight). You might spin round and try to punch the person (fight), or you might freeze on the spot. From a survival perspective, the hope would be that your reaction would either allow you to get away from the threat, overpower it, or make it lose interest.

But what happens to your thinking in that moment, when that hand goes on your shoulder? It might be that as you were walking home from your friend's house, you were thinking about what you were going to have as a snack when you got home, or whether you wanted to watch something before going to bed. But, as soon as that hand went on your shoulder, it's likely that your thoughts changed. Sometimes people find that it's as though their thoughts completely disappear, or they aren't thinking about anything anymore, or their thinking becomes narrowly focused on surviving that moment. When the threat system within our brain (the brainstem and amygdala) is activated, it bypasses or shuts down the 'thinking' part of our brain (the frontal cortex) which is just behind our forehead. The frontal cortex is the most developed and social part of our brain, and it's responsible for problem-solving, planning, reflecting, empathy and language. So, in a threat situation, our brain shuts down the parts of the brain that aren't essential, and instead focuses on the threat system. As with our tiger example, if we engaged with the thinking parts of our brain during a threat situation, this is likely to be unhelpful as by the time we had thought through the pros and cons of a potential reaction, we would probably have been attacked.

Traumatic memories

So, when we're experiencing a significant threat, our thinking brain goes 'offline'. This also has a big impact on how our brain processes our memories and what happens at this time.

There are two parts of our brain which have important roles in remembering: the hippocampus (or 'hippo' as we'll refer to it later in the book) and the amygdala. The amygdala spots potential threats in the environment and then tells your body how to react (setting off the fight/flight response). The amygdala focuses on the emotional and sensory parts of memories. They record how you felt, and what you saw, heard, smelt, tasted and your sense of touch (which are called 'somatic markers'), but not the facts or story of what happened. We sometimes talk about how trauma is stored within the nervous and sensory systems within the body. The amygdala can then easily be triggered by a sensory part of the memory (like a smell or taste), and when this happens you might suddenly experience a strong emotional response. For example, if you hear someone's voice before you see them, you might not quite know who it is at first but might still feel a sudden rush of happiness and find yourself smiling. There might be a song that reminds you of feelings of excitement or giddiness from a gig that you went to with friends, or a smell or taste that brings up feelings of cosiness or warmth from a childhood memory.

The hippo is a bit different, as it remembers the facts of what happened, and when and where something happened, but not the emotions associated with it or the sensory information. It remembers the story of what happened, and the process (i.e. this happened, then this happened, then this...) with the beginning, then middle and the end. Importantly, it remembers that the experience ended. We sometimes call this 'time-stamping' the memory – knowing when it happened, and that it's now ended.

So, usually, our brain takes the sensory and emotional information from the amygdala and puts it together with the factual and time-stamp information from the hippo, so that it can be filed away and processed. When we have both parts of the memory, it can be filed away but then brought back up when we need it or have something that reminds us of what happened.

But, when we're experiencing something traumatic, as we learned above, our thinking brain (which includes the hippo) goes offline. This means that our hippo is not working properly, so it can struggle to collate the facts of the situation (i.e. what actually happened) or time-stamp it. This can lead to us perhaps remembering fragments of what happened, but in a mixed-up order, with bits missing, and not even knowing that the traumatic experience has ended and we're safe again now. Also, our amygdala, which is part of the threat system, goes into overdrive when we're experiencing traumatic events. So, we might have lots of sensory and emotional information (we know how we felt and what we saw, smelt, touched, tasted, heard), but not know exactly what happened, and it can feel all a bit mixed up.

Our body and brain might not have worked out that the trauma ended, and we actually managed to survive it, as the hippo has been unable to give the memory a 'time-stamp' and the memories have not been filed away properly. So, the body and brain might think that the trauma is still happening, or is about to happen again, and they may continue to act as if it's happening again and they're still going through the traumatic event, even though it's ended, and they're now safe. So, sometimes the brain will continue to replay the traumatic event as if it's happening again in the here and now (through flashbacks, intrusive memories, night terrors) to try to process these fragmented memories. In order to get past this, the hippo needs to be trained to understand that the trauma ended, and is in the past, and that the person is safe now. Chapter 9 will talk about how to train your hippo to do this.

Dissociation as a coping and survival strategy

Lots of people dissociate a little in their everyday lives (such as zoning out or daydreaming occasionally), but when dissociation is a coping and survival strategy, the dissociative responses can be more extreme. Becoming cut off from what's happening in our surroundings and in our bodies can be a useful coping strategy to deal with trauma. This might be because we're experiencing over-whelming emotions following a traumatic event or it could be that during the difficult experience we couldn't use our other survival options, so we used a mental strategy to lessen the pain or distress from the situation (collapse). Dissociation protects our minds from the experience of our bodies.

We know that dissociation is more common when we can't action our 'fight or flight' response to remove ourselves from the physical or psychological danger and we're powerless and unable to fight back. If we can't run away and we can't fight the danger, we have to find some way to make it tolerable, and this can some-times be to escape in our heads and/or to cut off from the levels of stress our body is experiencing.

Dissociation can be described as a period of disconnection between your body and your brain. This disconnect can be wel-come and even pleasant if it alleviates our distress or anxiety, or it can be experienced as disturbing and unpleasant if we don't feel able to control it.

Beth describes her experience of dissociation:

It's not great when I zone out. I feel like I lose out on a lot because of it. It's like no time passes, but when I come back to, I have missed out on a lot. There's a lot of time when I zone out and I completely miss what's been going on around me and conversations that I should have known about. Zoning out is what I class as when I seem to detach from the world and others.

What does dissociation feel like?

Young people tell us that there are lots of different ways that they might experience the disconnection between their body and brain. Here are some of the things they describe:

- Feeling zoned out or disconnected from the world around you.

- Hands that don't feel as if they belong to you.

- Head that feels as if it's floating, not attached to the rest of your body.

- Zoning out during a conversation and not having any idea what's been said.

- An image in the mirror that doesn't feel as if it's actually you.

- A consuming feeling inside, a sense of losing control or coming apart.

- A daydream that is really very hard to snap out of.

- A period of time where it's really difficult to remember fully what has happened. Not remembering significant parts of your life.

- Unusual experiences such as hearing voices or sounds, seeing things that aren't there for a brief period of time.

Often after a period of dissociation you might feel drained and exhausted, even when you've not done anything to tire yourself out.

If it's a coping strategy, why can't you control it or choose when to use it?

Some people are able to use 'cutting off' consciously as a way to manage when things are overwhelming. Others seek help for feeling disconnected or dissociated because they no longer feel in control; they may feel scared or upset because it happens to them out of nowhere and makes them feel that they're losing control or going mad.

Children are much less able and likely to have the choice to simply get up and leave the home or school where they're being bullied, hurt or feeling really frightened. They may also be less physically able to fight the threat. An adult may be more able to walk away (although this can be tough for adults too) or fight back. This means that children are more at risk of being stuck in dangerous or scary situations without being able to action their fight or flight responses. It's therefore not surprising that dissociation often begins as a coping strategy in childhood. When this way of coping starts in response to a trauma early in life, then it's more likely to become an automatic response when the person is under stress in the future. This might be when it starts to feel out of control and unwanted.

What does it look like? (What might you and other people notice?)

For some of you, it might be hard for you or others to recognize when you're cut off and disconnected. It may just look as if you're daydreaming and not paying attention. For others, it may be really obvious as there are lots of physical changes that happen, including your eyes dilating, losing control of your posture (slump) and changes to your breathing (slowing down) and the colour of your skin (becoming paler). It's likely that your heart rate will slow right down, and you might notice that you still feel sweaty, but a cold sweat. You might notice that you're physically not feeling anything, or you may not feel pain. You might also struggle to interact with other people as you're so zoned out. People's physical changes can vary greatly. It's worth asking someone you know and trust and who you spend a lot of time with if they notice any changes in you when you feel disconnected. This can help you tell others what to look out for and what they can do to support you at these times of disconnection.

We sometimes call it the 'flop' response and some people actually do lose control of their posture and can physically look slumped or floppy too. Unlike when you're activated and ready to run or fight, this feels more like your body shutting down. It's really clever and helpful if you just have one occasion where this happens, as it protects you from feeling overwhelming distress and gives you some distance from a traumatic event. But if your body is relying on this way of coping with danger repeatedly throughout your childhood and possibly even into adulthood, then it can become a problem. It can also make people feel that they were 'not themselves' and didn't act in the way they would have liked/expected when something difficult or traumatic happened. For example, someone very caring may not have run to offer help because their body had shut down and they weren't able to think or act in the way they might under other circumstances. Chapter 9 focuses on grounding strategies, which are ways of helping us to feel more in control of dissociative reactions.

Flashbacks

Flashbacks are sometimes described as 'déjà vu', as if the traumatic experience is happening again in the here and now. Jake describes his flashbacks:

> They feel like I'm back at that moment again. I start to feel numb in my body, then I start zoning out, and I start to freeze... Déjà vu feels like you're not in the place you are at. For example, you're in your bed and you feel it coming. My body first goes numb. Then I zone out and feel like I am back at that memory, but I'm not there. Then I come back about 5–10 seconds later, my body still feels numb at first, but then it goes away.

During a flashback, our brain and body are reliving the traumatic experience in a way that feels so real. As we learned above, when we're processing traumatic memories, our hippo is working at a less than optimal level, which means that sometimes our brain doesn't know that the traumatic experience has actually ended, so we can continue to act (in our brain and body) as if the trauma is still happening or about to happen. We can also experience flashbacks as our brains try again and again to process the fragmented memories that may occur as a result of trauma.

Flashbacks can feel so real that it's as if they're taking over our experience in that moment, as in Lucy's example:

> I remember walking into my bedroom one day, and then my knees suddenly feeling weak, me falling forward unable to stand. Everything around me started to spin and I felt sick and like I was going to pass out. Tears were streaming down my face, I wasn't aware of them at first, but I could taste the saltiness in my mouth. I could see it happening. Again. It was like it was far away, but I could hear the sounds of the water splashing, I could hear the cruel

laughter, and I felt so scared, frozen to the spot. It was happening before me, but I couldn't do anything to stop it. Terrified. My chest felt like lead. I was struggling to breathe, panicking, gasping for breath. I grabbed at the first thing that I could and slid to the floor. I wanted it to stop. Now. My phone rang, it sounded so distant. But it persisted. I grabbed onto it and tried to answer. 'Help' I tried to say, but it came out as nothingness. 'Help' I tried again. I heard a friend's voice on the other end of the phone. 'You okay? What's happening?' I paused, mind all muddled, and tried to work out what was happening, I looked down and saw myself sat on the floor, tangled up in my duvet.

In this example, Lucy felt as if the trauma was happening to her again in that moment. Her memory of what happened was so strong that she could almost hear the sounds of water and laughter (associated with her trauma) and see again what happened in the past. In that moment, what was actually a strong memory felt as if it was happening in the here and now. But, when she heard her friend's voice on the phone, this brought her back to the present moment, and she was able to look around her and see that she was safe.

When Lucy experienced the flashback, it's likely that her memory had created a lot of stress in her body, with the same threat response being activated that was at the time of the initial trauma. This may have led her heart to start beating faster, her breathing to quicken, and her muscles to become tense, as occurred at the time of the traumatic experience. This might then have reinforced to her brain and body that she was unsafe and needed to protect herself as she did at the time of the traumatic event, for example by grabbing onto something or keeping low. In Chapter 9, we'll think about how to cope with and feel more in control of your flashbacks.

Unusual experiences

Sometimes we can hear and see things associated with a trauma even once we're safe. This can feel scary, as people may associate this with not being in touch with reality or being 'psychotic', but actually these experiences are much more common in people who are anxious or distressed and can be part of the way our brain processes trauma. Young people often tell us that they can hear the voice of an abuser or attacker, see a figure by the bed following abuse or a break-in, or feel things on their skin that aren't there. Jake shares his experience of hearing voices and seeing shadows:

> The voices scared me at first because I didn't know what was happening. But when they started saying to run away, I was like 'who said that?' because I didn't know where it came from. But then I started seeing shadow figures in the corners of my room like they were real people, and I was really scared because I didn't know what to do. But eventually I stopped seeing shadows. They were just in my head. They told me that they were real people and said that they had seen me before, and I believed that. Most of the time I could ignore them, but sometimes they would just stick around and keep saying it to me, so I listened to make them go away. But when I got told that they were not real, I calmed down and then eventually they started disappearing and I've not heard them for a while now.

We sometimes have unusual experiences partly because of the way our brain processes traumatic memories differently from every-day memories, and partly because we're experiencing significant distress.

Again, the meaning that we make of these experiences can be just as important as what actually happens. Just knowing that this is a result of trauma and likely to go away over time can be enough to make us feel less scared and make it less likely to happen again (as in Jake's example above). On the other hand, if we think this is a sign of serious mental illness and we're going to end up in hospital, this will only increase our distress and anxiety, and with increased stress comes a higher chance of us having the experience again, like a vicious circle. So, knowing these experiences are a trauma symptom and will pass can help us break this vicious circle.

Lola shares her experience:

> I was unlucky enough to walk into a place where a crime was being committed, and although I wasn't hurt, I was really scared and confused. I felt shaken and upset for a few days, but the thing that was really unnerving was when I was sat at home trying to relax and suddenly I heard a loud scream right in my ear. There was no one there. I knew it wasn't real, but I truly heard it with my own ears. Having knowledge about trauma and how it can affect you in lots of different and unusual ways meant that I was able to reassure myself I was going to be okay, but it was a reminder that it had a big impact and I needed to look after myself and let my friends and family know I might not be myself for a little while.

Dysregulation and distress

It's completely normal to feel overwhelmed by lots of big feelings following trauma. Distress is when there's so much going on in our bodies and at the same time we're trying to understand and make sense of what happened. It can sometimes feel as if our emotions dial has been 'turned up', and that small things can lead to big emotional responses. For example, sometimes watching a sad TV advert may lead you to start crying, or a friend might do something that you suddenly feel is incredibly irritating and might lead to you reacting angrily. These big emotional responses can also lead us to try to do whatever we can to feel okay again, and this can sometimes cause people to do things that might end up being unhelpful for them in the end (see Chapter 6 for more information about managing intense emotions). If we've been mostly safe and settled before the trauma, then these might be new feelings that we're not sure how to manage. If we've had to tolerate lots of traumatic events and haven't felt safe, then this can be an all too familiar feeling of being overwhelmed by feelings and unable to cope.

Jake talks about the dangers of bottling up emotions:

It's really hard for the person to cope... It's hard to say what's wrong, because you feel like no one would believe you. It can make people build up emotions inside them, and by not letting them out, they might run away or hurt themselves. And adults who don't know what's going on could get worried or not know what to do.

Hypersensitive threat system

We've talked above about what happens in the body and brain when we experience a traumatic experience. However, following a traumatic event, we might find that our body remains hyperaroused and threat-sensitive. This might mean that we feel on edge or jumpy, and our body has stayed ready to react, or we are easily triggered into a survival (fight/flight) response. If our body's survival response is triggered when there's no real threat, this leaves us with additional energy in the body (from the glucose released) but no way to use it up. This can mean that we feel restless, jittery, on edge, nervous and irritable.

Everyone is different

One thing that we know about trauma reactions is that everyone is different, and trauma can affect us in different ways. It might be that you recognize some of the above reactions in yourself, but not others. This is completely normal. But understanding your own reactions to what happened can be an important step to feeling more in control, and processing what happened to you.

♦ Chapter 3 ♦

Making Sense

We've told you a little about how trauma affects our brains and bodies in Chapter 2. In this chapter, we're going to think about how trauma affects how we think about the world, other people and most importantly ourselves. We are also going to think about how trauma affects our feelings and behaviour, because understanding this can reassure us that what we're experiencing is normal and part of a process of healing. But it can also be the source for intervention and starting to do things differently if we're feeling stuck and not recovering as we would hope or expect.

Cognitive behaviour therapy (CBT) is an evidence-based intervention for traumatic stress that helps the person to tell a coherent story about what happened to them (which can help to 'process' some of the fragmented memories – see Chapter 2). There is more information about CBT as a treatment option in Chapter 12. CBT looks at how some of the coping strategies that might have been helpful in the first place (like hiding away and avoiding things) have started to be a problem or have kept the problem going. It also helps the person to understand and challenge some of the impact of 'distorted thinking' after a trauma. The way we think about ourselves, other people and the world can be changed significantly by traumatic experiences, and we need to make sure that we're seeing things in a clear and balanced way rather than always through a hypervigilant lens looking for danger and threat.

We all have our own biases that affect how we see the world, which are based on a number of things including our life experiences. These biases provide 'short-cuts' for our brain and are really useful day to day. Some people may have *always* seen people as a potential threat and the world as frightening, because they grew up in a scary and unpredictable place. They are then likely to see future relationships, places and experiences through this lens, expecting them to be scary, unpredictable and untrustworthy too. If this is you, it may well be that you have to 'live what you learn' and have lots of experiences of safety and good relationships to change these beliefs. However, understanding and identifying your core (underlying) beliefs about yourself, other people and the world can help you to begin to be a little more flexible in how you see things (noticing when you're looking at things through this lens and choosing to challenge this a little – see below). It can also be useful to take time to really think through your own reactions and responses to see if they're *helpful* or *harmful*. This can simply be by asking yourself, 'Is what I'm doing right now helpful or harmful for me?', then deciding whether to carry on with it or not. It can also mean looking for the evidence and being a detective to see whether there are things that challenge your ideas. For example, if your experiences have left you believing that 'people are selfish and don't care about others', then you have this confirmed if someone doesn't hold a door open and catches you with it. But if you are open to looking for other evidence to the contrary, then you can take the time and notice the helpful smiling person asking if you are okay when the rude person doesn't hold the door open for you. This might make you recognize your bias and revise your thought to 'some people can be selfish but lots of people are there to help and do actually care'. CBT also tackles avoidance (both of thoughts and feelings and of places and people). Avoidance is one of the understandable coping strategies that we can develop following trauma that can then start to become part of the problem, and keep us trapped in feeling scared and powerless, or angry and alone (see Chapter 11 for how to tackle avoidance).

Shattered beliefs

We know that happy, confident people have beliefs about the world that are flexible and positive. For example, 'I'm a good enough person most of the time' and 'Other people usually like me', or 'Other people are pretty nice most of the time' and 'If something bad happens, I would have support and be able to cope with it'. When we experience a traumatic event, this can shatter all those beliefs and make us feel that 'I'm powerless' or 'Bad things will happen and there's nothing I can do to stop them'. These thoughts aren't 'true', they're just thoughts, but they're powerful and can provoke reactions in our body that create horrible anxious feelings. The anxious feelings in our body help convince us that those thoughts must be right, and that we feel terrible because everything is terrible.

Thoughts are **not** facts

It can sometimes be useful to try to remember that these thoughts are '*just* thoughts and *not* facts'. This might sound obvious to you or it might sound strange. Some of us will be good at holding lots of different ideas. But for others, especially if you are neuroatypical (with a diagnosis of autism, for example), and/or have experienced lots of early trauma, this kind of flexible thinking might be more difficult.

If we think 'I'm a horrible person' or 'People aren't safe', these thoughts are likely to have a big impact on how we feel, our relationships and connection with others and what we do. But, if we think 'I'm having the thought that I'm a horrible person. And I'm thinking that people aren't safe', it can help us to be able to step back and work out whether the thought is true, or whether it is biased thinking, based on what we've been through. It is time to be a detective and look at the evidence again to see if we can spot the things that might also suggest safety and support, rather than just the things that suggest danger and threat.

Attention

Part of the bias in our thinking is because of the impact on attention. To keep us safe after a traumatic event, or if we live somewhere dangerous, we start to pay attention to any potential threats in our environment, particularly those associated with the traumatic experience we went through. This is sometimes called 'hypervigilance', which is about being hyper-aware of our surroundings and always on the lookout for something going wrong. We can also call this 'meerkat brain' as we can be like that meerkat on the top of the hill, ignoring all the worms and their friends playing because their job is looking for threats. When we are always looking out for potential threats, it's hard to 'switch off'. Partly, this is a survival strategy as our brain tunes in to danger to keep us safe and we don't know that we're doing it. But we can also be purposefully paying attention to things that are related to our trauma to try to understand what happened to us and to make sure it never happens again. For example, if you were in a car accident, you might look a lot at the internet and read all the news stories about crashes that have happened. People around can find this hard to understand, but it's normal to want to understand and make sense of what's happened to you. Seeking out information like this can be one way that we try to cope with traumatic experiences because we think if we know all the facts about car crashes, when and why they happen, then this can stop it happening to us ever again.

'Seeking out' is the opposite of 'avoidance', which we talk about below and in Chapter 11, but can be just as problematic as it can keep your attention focused on danger, ignoring signs of safety, and can also keep your body activated and ready for threat when you're actually safe. If you were hurt by another person, you may find that you're watching other people closely, looking for signs of anger, rejection and dishonesty, and reasons not to trust them too. This often means that you find it hard to get close to or trust other people, even if they're safe. Limiting your time on the internet and being aware of the kind of information you're seeking out can be helpful. Also, you may talk to your trusted adult a lot about what happened and ask lots of questions and want reassurance. This is totally normal, but it might be that it's also keeping your attention and focus on the traumatic event. So, you might want to agree with them that they only offer the reassurance once or twice, then they encourage you to do a positive activity that will hold your attention.

Avoidance

When we feel anxious and afraid, avoidance is a common coping strategy. If we believe that the world is dangerous, and we can't control it, then it's better to just stay at home and not put ourselves in danger, right?

A period of rest and recuperation following a traumatic event is our body's natural response and can help us to process the trauma and heal. In basic evolutionary terms, we might think we've developed to 'go and hide in our cave until the dangerous predator or disease that killed others has moved on'. But if this becomes our main coping strategy over an extended period of time, then we've got a problem. Avoidance, whether this be staying at home or avoiding other people, means we miss out on opportunities to learn that the world is mostly safe even though bad things can happen. We don't get to see the caring people who want to connect and help us heal, so we continue to be preoccupied with the traumatic event, or the person who hurt us, or our thoughts about how we were powerless and unable to prevent the traumatic event or events happening.

We talk about how to avoid avoidance in Chapter 11. It's important that you have enough time to let your body and brain do what they need to do (Chapter 2), and it can be helpful to take time to reflect on what you're thinking, what's going on in your body and what you and the people around you can do to help and make you feel okay. Get back into some sort of routine, take care of yourself and find what helps to calm down your threat system and helps you feel okay and safe (see Chapter 5 for the basics of self-care and Chapter 6 for ways to self-soothe and calm). Once you've got some of these structures and coping strategies in place, it's important to start to slowly take steps to face things that might be associated with your trauma and have an impact on your daily life. Some things associated with our traumatic experiences we might just about be able to face a couple of times with some support. Other things may be more difficult and we might need to take a more gradual approach to facing our fears and things that might trigger our trauma reactions.

BRIDIE – PERSONAL EXPERIENCE

When I was working in a hospital something traumatic happened to a young person in one of the rooms on the ward and it upset me a lot. For a few weeks, I couldn't walk down a part of the ward and so would walk the long way round every time. Even the thought of walking through the door to that part of the ward made me feel sick and start to sweat. My thoughts would race and get all jumbled. I didn't want to worry the young people or my colleagues, so I avoided it for ages. I pretended to myself that it wasn't a big deal and didn't matter. I mentioned it to a psychologist that I trust, and they were understanding and supportive but also told me that I had to start to go down there to see that I may get upset or have some thoughts and feelings that were unpleasant and overwhelming but that I could cope, and they would be there to talk to if I felt overwhelmed. I tell the young people that I work with about facing their fears all the time, but when the emotions and sensations are overwhelming, sometimes the avoiding behaviour doesn't feel like a big deal – 'It's not that far to go around', but really it is keeping the trauma alive in the present when it isn't and doesn't need to be.

Cognitive avoidance (not thinking about what's happened)

We can even try to avoid thinking about the traumatic event/s or things associated with it. We call this 'cognitive avoidance'. To do this, we might avoid any people or places that remind us of the event and try to keep busy all the time so we can't think about what happened to us and don't have to experience the horrible feelings and reactions that can happen when we think about it. This makes sense, right? If thinking about it makes you feel awful, then just don't think about it.

The problem is that this simply doesn't work. For example, try not to think about pink elephants for a minute or two. What happens? That's right, pink elephants seem to be everywhere and it's so hard not to think about them! Even if you might be able to ignore them for a minute, they're likely to start popping up again after that. When we set the goal 'Don't think about X', then our brain is set up to monitor whether or not we've achieved that goal. So, it checks, 'Have you thought about X?', which means that it actually can end up popping into our heads more often. While we're suppressing and avoiding the thoughts, we're not able to make sense of, and tell the story of, what happened to us as an event that happened in the past and is over. It can feel overwhelming to face what's happened and begin to tell the story. It's important that we don't rush it, but step by step we need to start testing out our ability to face our thoughts and memories. It can be important to involve others, and sometimes you might feel you need to reach out to a trained therapist to help you to navigate that process (see Chapter 12 for information about further therapy).

Developmental trauma and how it affects our thoughts, feelings and behaviour

If we have experienced repeated trauma in our childhoods and within our relationships with people who are caring for us, then this has a significant impact on how we see ourselves, other people and the world (see Chapter 4 for more on this). We may not be aware of these beliefs as we go about our lives day to day, and we are simply acting according to our 'instincts'. Karen Treisman, an author and trainer in developmental trauma, talks about children who have grown up in scary environments as though they have been in shark-infested waters where there may also be dolphins and seaweed, but they always know that there is danger around. It makes sense to always be on the lookout for danger, to either make yourself tiny or hide because sharks are too big to fight off. Rather than marvelling at the lovely dolphins, instead it's helpful to have a threat response to every movement and to stay still and watch and be careful. If we take a person who has grown up in these shark-infested waters and put them in a swimming pool, will they suddenly start to play without any fear? No! Of course not. They'll still be on the lookout for sharks and stay tuned in to every movement as danger. If we grow up in danger, then our body and brain learn to survive. But this might not fit so well once we're out of the danger and in a safe place, maybe a new home or away from someone who has not been able to keep us safe and take care of us. It may be that your shark-infested water was a house where there was a lot of shouting and domestic abuse, but now you live just with safe people in a safe place – but you know that the way you think about things and the way that you respond (especially to others) doesn't just change to 'safe mode'. Even though you are now in a safe place, you continue to be tuned in to all the same threats and cues of danger. A raised voice might now be someone calling you down for dinner, but your heart rate still rises and you think 'It's all kicking off', and it takes some time for your threat response to calm down and for you to realize you are safe and can go down and eat your tea.

Beth discusses her experience:

> Being in a traumatic relationship has caused me to build up walls that shouldn't be there. I feel like I sometimes find it very difficult to build new relationships with people because of how little trust I have now. I also feel like I can't tell the people closest to me things about myself as I feel they will use it against me like in my past relationship.

When we've experienced a lot of trauma in our early lives and this has led us to develop threat-related core beliefs (e.g. 'I'm not safe', 'Others are unpredictable and not to be trusted' and 'The world is a scary and hostile place'), it can be helpful to think about our early and important experiences and understand where these beliefs come from and how they might impact our coping and relationships in the here and now. Without this, it can be really hard to think about what we need to start to feel safe again. Looking for evidence and being aware that thoughts are not facts is still helpful, but we might need to think more deeply about how to get the experiences of safety and connection that we need to be able to do this.

Telling your story and making sense of what's difficult

One of the hardest parts of making sense of your story is to identify the 'core pain' or 'key fears' that have developed due to your experiences and that drive your coping strategies. We talk about 'coping in the best way you know how' because we really believe that even behaviours that might be defined as dysfunctional or self-destructive are usually just people trying to cope with their traumatic experiences. Sometimes these behaviours are a way that the person is trying to feel safe and okay in their bodies, and cope and stay safe in their relationships.

Often the problem can be that the strategies have unintended consequences, which can sometimes lead to you feeling even worse. For example, avoiding even thinking about what happened can lead to more intrusive thoughts and nightmares and fearing that you might explode or upset others. Frequently seeking out information about the traumatic event can lead you to be constantly in a state of anxiety and arousal.

This process of telling a story to try to find the best way to help is what psychologists call 'formulation'. Other people might call it 'telling my story'. Trying to make sense of the impact of the trauma on your thoughts, feelings and coping strategies in this way can be the best place to start to make a plan to recover from your traumatic experience/s and find healthy sustainable ways to manage the big feelings that trauma has left you with.

It's really important to be thoughtful and compassionate about where your coping strategies come from, and then use these stories to find new, more helpful and healthy ways to manage your feelings and responses as well as your relationships. You can also use them to help the people around you to understand the impact of trauma and some of your responses and then how they might be able to help and support you.

What's happened to you?

The first step of understanding is to think about your early experiences and how these might have impacted how you feel about yourself, other people and the world. You can then think about whether the traumatic event was part of your early experiences (developmental trauma) or if the traumatic event has changed your core beliefs and made you think differently.

What are you really scared of?

If you can work out what core pain you're trying to avoid or protect yourself from, then this can help you to understand your coping strategies and what imagined threat (that you're really fearful of happening) they're helping you to avoid or reduce. This is about figuring out how the things that have happened to you have shaped what you're concerned about, or even scared of, in the here and now. For example, often if you've experienced a lot of loss or moving around, then the key fear might be that people will leave you, and you'll end up abandoned and alone. This fear can often be easily activated – maybe goodbyes or if your partner didn't put their usual kiss at the end of their message. If you've been bullied at school, then the key fear or concern might be that other people are going to criticize, reject or humiliate you – this fear could be triggered by something as simple as a funny look or passing comment.

It's important to think about both the external fears (such as others hurting or leaving you) and internal fears (like being overwhelmed by your feelings or difficult memories) as they're both important 'threats' that you'll cope with in different ways.

Coping in the best way you know how...

Depending on your experiences and the key fears that these have left you with, you'll have found ways to avoid these threats and feel okay when they're overwhelming. It might be that you use eating lots of sweet food, drinking alcohol or smoking cigarettes to try to manage or avoid intense feelings, or that you push people away when they get close to avoid the pain of them rejecting you. You may isolate yourself and be aloof, so you don't have to worry about putting your trust in other people. It could be that you cope with your fear of not being good enough by constantly striving to be the best and 'perfect' in your relationships and work.

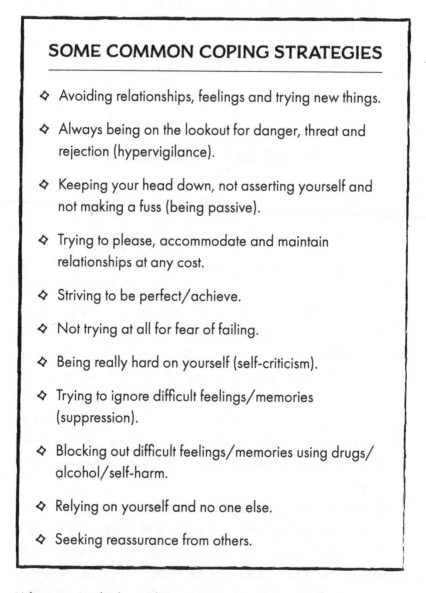

SOME COMMON COPING STRATEGIES

◇ Avoiding relationships, feelings and trying new things.

◇ Always being on the lookout for danger, threat and rejection (hypervigilance).

◇ Keeping your head down, not asserting yourself and not making a fuss (being passive).

◇ Trying to please, accommodate and maintain relationships at any cost.

◇ Striving to be perfect/achieve.

◇ Not trying at all for fear of failing.

◇ Being really hard on yourself (self-criticism).

◇ Trying to ignore difficult feelings/memories (suppression).

◇ Blocking out difficult feelings/memories using drugs/alcohol/self-harm.

◇ Relying on yourself and no one else.

◇ Seeking reassurance from others.

When you're thinking about coping strategies that you might use, it can be useful to have someone who knows you well to help you. When you've been using a strategy for a long time it can be hard to see where it comes from or link it to your fears as it just becomes 'what you do'. Remember that if you tend to be self-critical (perhaps as a way of protecting yourself), this can make it even more difficult when you're looking at how you cope. Be aware of any 'should' or 'should nots' creeping in. You need to be able to recognize these and be compassionate to yourself, as these are understandable responses to dealing with your fears and you were just coping in the best way that you knew how.

Unintended consequences

We're pretty clear that these coping strategies made sense at some point in your lives and also often may have made you feel better right away. For example, if you tell the person you really like that you don't want to hang out with them again, then you might feel an initial flood of relief that you don't have to tolerate the anxiety of waiting and expecting them to reject you. But over time you might start to feel sad about missing them and even angry with yourself for not giving them (and you) a chance at the relationship developing.

If you start to feel angry because a friend really let you down and then choose to suppress it, ignore it and be passive not to upset your friend, then you don't have to deal with the anger or difficult interaction. But then they do it *again*. Now you're twice as angry at them and also angry at yourself. These are the unintended consequences.

Sometimes coping strategies work well at avoiding the feared outcome, but they also reinforce the unhelpful ideas we have about ourselves, other people and the world and keep us trapped in the same patterns of behaviour and the same kinds of relationships. For example, if you push people away to keep yourself safe, then you will undoubtedly have fewer people in your life and so the ideas 'I'm not lovable' and 'Other people aren't there for me' are strengthened and there are even more reasons to hide away – you're stuck in a vicious cycle.

One way of thinking about this is to consider how holly leaves react when they are under threat of being eaten. Holly leaves, believe it or not, are naturally smooth and rounded at the edges. However, they're primed to change shape and become prickly and spiky if they are in a place where they're likely to be nibbled at by animals. This spikiness makes the animals stay away and not eat the leaves. Humans can also learn to become spiky and find ways to keep other people away if they're scared that they'll get hurt (such as saying nasty things, pushing people away or rejecting them). But this keeping people away from us can also make us feel lonely and isolated. And it can keep us feeling afraid of others and still believing that we would get hurt (even if the people now trying to get close to us are safe and wouldn't 'nibble our leaves').

Protective factors

The things that make us feel good, alive and connected are often key to learning to manage intense emotions, so it's important to spend some time reflecting on and recording what exactly these things are. They could be personal qualities (e.g. I can laugh at myself) or they might be activities that you enjoy (e.g. yoga or playing football). Again, asking for help from a key adult or friend can help, or simply ask yourself, 'What would [insert name of favourite friend/carer/teacher] say has kept me strong and what would they recognize as my best qualities?'

Putting it all together

In the box below, there's a template for writing your own formulation or story (and there is a blank copy that you can download in Appendix II) and we hope that this helps you to try and move away from 'What's wrong with me?' to thinking about 'What's happened to me? And how has this made me feel and then shaped how I'm coping with my feelings now?' This provides us with a good starting point for working out what's going to help and what strategies we can try to feel more in control of our feelings and happier in our relationships.

MY STORY

What's happened to me? (What are my life experiences?) (e.g. being bullied, arguments at home, being attacked, not being looked after)

What am I really scared of? (What pain/fear might I be trying to avoid or protect myself from?) (e.g. that other people will leave me, and I'll end up abandoned and alone, that people will criticize, reject or humiliate me, being hurt/attacked again, feeling vulnerable, or my emotions (or memories) being too overwhelming or out of control)

What am I doing to cope in the best way I know how? (What am I doing to cope with the fears above? How am I protecting myself against them?) (e.g. keeping others close to me/seeking reassurance that they care OR keeping others at a distance and coping by myself, always being on the lookout for potential threats, doing whatever I can to make people like me, trying to ignore or block out

---

my difficult feelings (including drinking) or not trying things so that I don't risk failing at them)

What are the unintended consequences of my ways of coping? (e.g. people get frustrated with me and pull away, which leads to me feeling even more rejected and let down, OR my emotions build up and then I get suddenly angry/ aggressive, I end up feeling really bad about myself and more anxious because of drinking, or people end up taking advantage of me)

What are my protective factors? (What helps me to cope in a positive way/feel better?) (e.g. running/exercise helps me a lot, talking to my aunty who I feel that I can trust. My friends are a good distraction when I'm struggling)

Chapter 4

Connection and Disconnection

Relationships are complicated and trauma is complicated. In this chapter, we're going to think about how the way you relate to (interact or connect with) other people can affect how you recover after trauma, and also how trauma can change the way you relate to people. Sometimes our ways of relating can lead us to feeling disconnected from other people, when we most need their care and support.

One important definition of trauma is feeling scared *and alone*. Being alone can be one of the most powerful parts of difficult experiences and have an effect on how we feel about others long after we're in a much safer place. Young people often talk about feeling disconnected from others after a traumatic event or when they've had lots of difficult experiences in their early lives.

We often hear young people (and adults) say that they're okay on their own and they don't need anyone else. Being independent and a 'coper' is really valued in most Western cultures, especially for boys and men. Despite this, what we know is that coping alone is just not the way that humans are hardwired. Our different experiences and styles of relating mean some of us are more likely to want to try to manage things on our own, whereas others feel more comfortable relying on and looking for the support of others. There's no right or wrong, they're just different. What we know is that people who are resilient and overcome trauma are flexible and can move easily between different ways of relating and coping when they need to. They don't get stuck and rely on old patterns when they aren't helpful or are even harmful.

To help us think how you might seek support and how trauma might have affected your relationships, we're going to introduce you to the four different ways that we know people relate to others based on their early experiences. These are what psychologists would call 'attachment styles'. In reality, we often have a mix of attachment styles, they change over time, and the way we relate changes depending on who we're in the relationship with...but for the sake of keeping things understandable and trying to work out what you need right now, we'll talk about them as four categories.

Attachment styles

Secure attachment

Stevie is usually pretty easy for others to get along with. They're okay on their own but can ask for help when they need it. When Stevie was little, the adults in their life were there when they needed them – most of the time. The adults looked out for clues about what Stevie needed, enjoyed spending time with them but also encouraged Stevie to get out there and explore the world and were pleased and excited when they did this. Stevie generally likes themselves, thinks that other people are pretty nice really, bad things don't just pop up out of nowhere, and that they can cope with most things. If things get too much, they know that there will be someone who can help them out and make them feel okay again.

Anxious or preoccupied attachment

Alex is often worried about other people and whether adults are going to be there when they need them, or if people will reject them if they get things wrong. Alex might test adults out to make sure they'll be there when they need them, even if they don't need them right now. For example, they may say something vague about not being okay to make other people feel worried and so they do not forget about them. Alex can get quite preoccupied with friendships and relationships, and other people might find them quite intense. This intensity can freak friends out a bit and mean Alex's worst fears come true and people distance themselves. When Alex was little, adults weren't always there for them. Because Alex wasn't sure when/if adults were going to be able to meet their needs, they learned to keep adults' attention as much as they possibly could, and this became more of a focus than getting out there to explore. Alex might exaggerate things a bit to make sure people are taking notice, but this can also make people doubt whether these feelings and needs are real. Alex thinks that the world is scary and that they aren't safe unless someone is there to keep them safe and make them feel okay.

Avoidant attachment

Ari seems confident and easy to get along with, but rarely asks for help or lets other people see what it's really like to be them. Ari doesn't like being vulnerable. Ari is focused on achieving and getting things done and doesn't really have time for feelings or investing in relationships. Ari feels okay about themselves. They believe that the world is to be explored, and they can look after themselves. But they also believe that other people aren't to be trusted and so are best kept at arm's length. Ari doesn't let others know what they think or feel because Ari believes other people will only hurt you or let you down. When Ari was little, adults didn't come when they cried or respond to what they needed, so Ari learned to look after themselves. Ari thinks that if they told other people they needed something, other people would reject and/or laugh at them, or ignore their needs, so they keep quiet and rely on themselves.

Aubrey is also avoidant. They respond like Ari, but for them it was because the adults in their life got really upset when Aubrey got upset and really angry when Aubrey got frustrated. They couldn't let Aubrey feel their negative feelings, they found that too upsetting, so they overreacted and made Aubrey withdraw. So Aubrey learned just to keep these feelings hidden and rely on themselves to cope.

Disorganized attachment

Darby was a lovable baby who ended up with parents or carers who were either very scared, or very scary. This made it impossible for Darby to get any comfort when they needed it because the adults who should be making them feel okay were the ones causing Darby to feel scared. Darby wants to connect with others just as we all do, but they can find it almost unbearable to be close to others, so they try to control the environment instead. Darby might seem controlling, they may control things around them and people, and need things to be 'just so', struggle with change or the unexpected, or even lash out and hurt others or harm themselves to keep people away. Darby doesn't feel okay and they can neither let others help them feel okay nor make themselves feel okay. Darby is really stuck and struggling.

Your attachment style

Do you recognize yourself in any of these descriptions? It may well be that you're mostly secure but at times of stress you feel like you are only okay if you can be with someone safe. Or that you're mostly avoidant and keep people at a distance, coping well, but sometimes you feel really overwhelmed and do things that you really regret like hurting others or yourself, and feel really stuck. No one fits in the box completely, but it can be helpful to think, 'What do I do when I feel stressed?' Have a think about this for a few minutes and reflect on times when you've felt overwhelmed or have experienced difficult things.

Did you hide away from others and try to avoid them by staying in your room? Did you immediately seek out comfort and reassurance by calling someone you trust? Did you feel paralysed by stress and end up doing things you later regretted, or others found hard to understand? Be kind to yourself when you are thinking about these things, as it is tough.

If your early life was very difficult and you had to move between different carers or your main carers were scary, then this often has a big impact on how you respond when life gets tough – and especially on how much trust you can put in others to help you. Psychologists sometimes call this a 'double disability' because you have more pain, separation and loss so need support and care to heal and feel okay, but also have a mistrust in others and a fear of relationships that make you less likely to be able to get what you need from others. This is not something you should be trying to tackle on your own. You need lots of experiences with adults who are safe and consistent and show you care when you need it to be able to learn what you need to live and feel safe in your body. That doesn't mean that you can't use some of the ideas in this book to learn to manage your trauma responses, but it does mean you might want to look carefully at Chapter 3 and think about whether you might like to start working with an adult you trust to try to make sense of your story together.

It's important to remember that the way you relate to others developed to keep you safe and help you survive when you were little. Be kind to yourself and remember that these patterns or 'dances' can feel really difficult to step out of, but it's always possible to develop new ways of seeking support and getting your needs met by the important people in your life. You can start to do this by being aware of what you do and 'taking a pause' to think about what you really need and what will be most helpful for you at times of stress. Following a traumatic experience or when you've experienced lots of trauma in your early life, being aware of how you're thinking and feeling about yourself and others is the important first step to finding more helpful and healthy ways to seek support and feel heard and seen. Being heard, telling your own story and feeling seen and important are crucial parts of healing and recovery after trauma.

Why do we need to connect?

Our attachment system is what drives us to connect with others and seek support and comfort. Support from another person is one of the quickest ways our bodies return to normal after something stressful or traumatic happens. A long time ago, some psychologists showed that holding the hand of someone who cares about them meant that people reported less pain while being given an electric shock (yes, psychologists used to do some really terrible experiments on people!). When they measured different signs of stress in their bodies as well as just what people told them about the pain, their stress responses were also lower (lower heart rate and blood pressure). People experienced the most physical stress and reported the worst pain if they were alone when they got the electric shock. But even a stranger holding their hand made it less painful and their bodies showed less stress. Human contact and connection are one of the best ways to calm our stress response and let us get back to exploring the world.

So, our in-built drive to connect with others and have them see and understand what has happened to us can calm our threat response and make us feel okay again. On a day-to-day basis, we see this in why many people will call the person they trust most and who cares for them when something bad happens or if they get bad news. We want to be close to our special person and someone who can make us feel safe and okay again, and then once we're soothed, we can go back to getting on with our day, learning and doing.

We hope that you're reading this book feeling that you still have trust in others and the important people who you feel safe with and you know can make you feel better. If you don't, then let's have a think about what's getting in the way and what we might do to help you get back previous connections you had or start to make new ones.

What gets in the way of others being able to make us feel better after difficult experiences?

If you're mostly secure like Stevie...

If you believe that you're okay, other people are pretty nice really and that the world is mostly an interesting and safe place, then a traumatic event like an accident or an assault can make you doubt everything and shake your core beliefs (see Chapter 3). You may suddenly only feel okay if you're with someone else and not feel as if you can cope alone when usually you feel confident to do this. Alternatively, you may feel that you can't share your thoughts and feelings with people around you like you normally would, because you suddenly feel different and are struggling to trust people or believe that they can connect with what's going on inside you. Everything feels different and your trust is shaken.

If you're mostly avoidant like Ari or Aubrey

If you're avoidant, then probably when stressful things have happened before, you've felt able to manage alone. This means when you experience a trauma and actually need help to feel okay, you don't know how to approach people and ask for help. You probably don't have the words to let them know what's going on inside you either (or you might not even know how you feel yourself because you're so used to pretending you don't have feelings). It's likely that adults generally leave you alone when you're upset as they know that you tend to just come round without much help. It can also feel really uncomfortable to ask for help and can make you feel anxious or even ashamed. Because you've got good at keeping feelings to yourself then others can't see distress and don't realize that you're struggling or suffering. This can then leave you feeling lonely and that no one understands you. Often the feelings start bursting out in big angry or emotional ways because it's not possible to keep them to yourself anymore. Like a bottle of fizzy drink that has been shaken, you can only keep the lid on for so long. If you're not letting the feelings out, then sooner or later the lid will come flying off. When you do show your feelings and it's a big outburst, this might make you feel embarrassed and/or adults really worried about you, and their concern feels too much and makes you shut down again.

If you're mostly anxious like Alex...

If you often need support to feel better but struggle to trust that support, then it can be tough following a traumatic event. You may feel that any coping skills you've developed over the years aren't enough and you need others to be there and help you to feel okay. This becomes a problem mostly when there's not someone who can be there with you when you need them or when others start to feel overwhelmed by how much you need them. You might be testing other people out all the time to make sure that people know you're not okay. You might also want to test out that you can rely on them all the time by telling them how awful it feels, showing them how awful it feels, or by shutting them out completely to see if they'll come and seek you out and make sure you're okay.

What else fuels disconnection?

When trauma disrupts our usual ways of seeking comfort or feeling okay, then we can feel disconnected both from others and our sense of ourselves and who we are.

If something traumatic happened to you alone then you can suddenly feel disconnected as your friends and family are struggling to understand or know what to do (because they haven't been through anything similar). Alternatively, it might be that your family or friends were part of the same traumatic event but are coping with it differently. If you're wanting to take some time to think it through alone and they want to keep talking about what happened, then this can be painful and make you feel overwhelmed. If they're unable to talk about what happened and you cope by talking things through, then this can cause tension and a feeling that you're 'walking on eggshells' so as not to say the wrong thing or even mention it. Or you might end up feeling worried about 'burdening' them with your own struggles, if you can see that they're struggling too, even when you might really need their support. It's not unusual for different people who went through the same thing to deal with it differently, and no way is 'right'.

Connection heals

We know that when someone we trust can allow you to share your experiences in a way that feels right for you and you are able to make sense of what happened together, this is one of the best ways to heal after trauma and feel safe again. It doesn't matter if that person had the same experience or not if you feel safe and heard.

It's important that the adults around you understand what you need so they can provide support in a way that you can access and accept it. We asked a group of young people who had been through some difficult experiences what they wished the adults (including professionals) had known when they were supporting them through trauma. We talked about what was helpful and what was meant to be helpful but was actually quite difficult or unhelpful.

These ideas and answers were taken from these conversations.

We hope they can provide pointers or just conversation starters for the people who are around and supporting you. They may ask you what you need or what they can do. It could be good to highlight the ones that you feel most apply to you and let them have a look! Even if they don't ask, be brave and show them anyway. Connection is the route to healing and we're rooting for you and all the adults who are supporting you.

I wish that the adults had known that...

- even as a teenager with lots of friends it can be hard to talk to them about traumatic experiences, so adults might be the only people who I can share my thoughts and feelings with

- just because you are a grown-up doesn't mean you have to fix things or have the answer. The people who help the most are just easy to talk to – people who are easy to talk to don't butt in or interrupt, they just sit and listen and say 'I want to help' or 'I am so glad you told me' but don't pretend they have all the answers or can make it all better

- to be able to talk to you I need to know for sure that you are interested and care about my feelings – even the difficult ones. I know this when you are available to me and ask about me and what is going on in my life

- often I am struggling to understand what is happening, so please don't ask 'Why?' when I do or say things. It can feel as if you are judging me

- when people say 'You should talk to X about this' (e.g. your therapist or a certain teacher) it can feel as if you don't want to talk to me

- where we talk always needs to feel safe and be private and away from others – the place is nearly as important as the person (but not as important)

– too many questions can feel too much and make me shut down

– sometimes talking doesn't help and I need support in another way, like eating together or watching a movie together. Doing things and playing games can help me calm down just as much as talking

– trying to make things better can often make things feel worse. We just want to be listened to and to know that you are there. We don't want to be told that things are going to be okay because that can feel impossible to believe when something really bad has happened

– when you don't always have time for me it can then feel hard to talk at the 'right' time when you are free

– I don't want lots of small talk that can feel dismissive, but I also need you to be careful about talking directly about the past because that can be too much and cause me to have trauma reactions like flashbacks and become disconnected or even dissociated

– you really need to know and understand me before you start making links between what is going on now and what happened in the past because I feel upset and not understood when adults get this wrong.

There is a summary of these ideas that you can download in Appendix III. Maybe you can share these with some important people in your life to help them to know how to support you or even just to get that conversation started and begin to think about what you need together.

Top tips for safe connection

Once you've identified the way you usually relate, and then the way that you think your traumatic experiences may have affected your relationships, take some time to think about what you really need.

The coping strategies that you focus on or spend the most time on as you read this book will be impacted by your attachment style and the sort of trauma that you have experienced.

Do you struggle to feel safe alone? Then maybe practise doing some of the self-soothe strategies in Chapter 6 for a few minutes, or some movements like those in Chapters 7 and 8, before you go downstairs and get an adult or before you pick up the phone. Just start to practise in small ways doing things to make you feel okay and show yourself that you can do it without someone there – some of the time.

Do you struggle to ask for help? Then maybe you need to think about how you're going to let adults know that you're not okay. You might not have done this before. You need to work out who you feel can be there for you without being too much, and then work out a way to let them know when you might need their time/support. Maybe a text message or a note rather than a conversation if this feels overwhelming. Some people like to have a code word that lets someone in their house know that they need to be together. It can also be useful to think about what you want from them at the time. Sometimes we might just want to be physically close to someone or to have a hug; other times we might want to talk things through. Or we might want them to play a game with us or watch a TV show. It can be helpful to let the person know what we would find useful, so that they know how to help us, and we can feel safer about their response. Try writing this down and developing a 'support plan' when you are feeling calm and okay and then share it when you are feeling overwhelmed or unsure, as it is much harder to talk when you are already feeling upset.

It may be tempting to seek support online from people you don't have to look at every day or even look in the face at all. We would ask that you be super careful about this as it can expose you to further trauma, either by accident (people triggering your trauma reactions with their own story) or through people exploiting young people who are sharing difficult experiences to get their own needs met.

We hope that using the ideas from this chapter about how you might be responding to others based on your primary attachment style and/or the way you have responded since you experienced trauma will help you to navigate the rest of this book and find the strategies that are most likely to fuel connection and make you feel secure and supported as we know that this is the key to healing and feeling safe again.

◇ Chapter 5 ◇

Getting the Basics Right: Enhancing Safety and Stabilization

This is the fourth book we have written for young people and young adults about managing difficult feelings. In every book, we take some time to talk about 'getting the basics right'. We do this because we know that this is the foundation for recovery and getting or staying healthy. Without taking care of our body and our basic needs, we're going to struggle to think straight and stay motivated for some of the more complicated things that we talk about in other chapters.

Making sure you're safe

One of the most important messages that we wanted to get across in this book is that the first thing that you need to do to cope with trauma is to make sure that you're no longer experiencing the trauma. For example, if you're in a relationship (with a parent, friend or partner) where you're continuing to be hurt, the most important thing is *not* to learn how to cope with this, but to get out of it.

It's NEVER okay for someone to feel unsafe, or worried about their safety, in a relationship. Although it can sometimes feel scary to be able to get away or ask for help, or we might even feel that we don't deserve to, it's the most important thing to do.

If the trauma hasn't stopped, please do tell someone safe (someone close to you, such as a trusted adult, or someone on a helpline/support service), so that they can support you to get help and get out of the traumatic situation. There are a lot of helplines and support services that are there to help you if you're still stuck experiencing trauma. They're trained in this stuff and will have helped a lot of other people in a similar position to you, so they'll get it, and will have ways to help you. In Appendix IV, there's a list of helplines and websites from the UK (where the authors of this book are from).

Telling someone

We know that it's not always easy to tell someone what's going on. You might worry about what they will say, whether they will be able to help, or what they will think about you. Sometimes people also worry that what they have been through might seem silly or trivial to other people (even though it isn't), or that it's too much and the other person won't be able to cope with it. So, take care of yourself, and maybe think about who to tell (e.g. someone close to you, or a helpline), and how to tell them (e.g. a message or in person). According to Jake:

> It feels a bit scary at first, but once you start talking it gets a bit better, and when you have said it, you feel prouder of yourself for telling someone how you feel, and it makes you more confident to tell more things that you can remember... Speaking to people

has made me feel happier, because I'm saying how I feel and they understand.

When we asked Reggie what his biggest message for young people reading this book was, he said:

You're not alone. There's always someone to talk to if you ask for help. Give it a go, otherwise you're carrying it around with you, and it will eventually pull you down and you'll end up feeling worse about yourself.

Basic safety

When you're feeling unsafe, this might be because something traumatic has happened recently, or because you're still feeling unsafe from something that happened a long time ago. Either way, there are things that you can do to increase your feelings of safety and stability.

It can be useful to ask yourself the following questions:

- Is my environment safe? Is there anything that I can do that might make my home/room/space feel safer?

- Are my basic needs being met? Am I eating properly? Do I have somewhere to sleep? Do I have someone to talk to?

- Am I looking after myself well enough, such as making sure that I'm sleeping properly, washing myself and taking care of my appearance, exercising, doing things that I enjoy?

- Can I get through a 'normal' day for me – getting up, washing, eating, getting to school/college or work, seeing friends?

- Have I got enough structure in my day-to-day life? For example, do I have a time to get up, something meaningful to do in the day (such as going to school, college or work), proper mealtimes, a bedtime?

- When I'm feeling upset, anxious or overwhelmed, am I able to help myself to feel better?

- Do I have people around me who support me to feel okay?

- Do I have everyday activities that I enjoy, or where I have fun?

- Do I feel able to manage the trauma reactions that I experience, or does it feel as if they are in control of me?

- Am I experiencing any ongoing threats?

This might sound like a silly thing to say, but it's really important that the bad stuff or trauma is as resolved as it can be for now. For example, if you were physically assaulted, any injuries need to have healed, and you now feel safe from the person who attacked you, either because they have been locked up, you now live far away from them, or your home environment is safe (e.g. house alarm, locks on the door).

Then after that, the next step is starting to put back and strengthen any basic building blocks, like the ones in the questions above, to start to build back your safety and stability.

Getting the basics right

Some people are generally good at taking care of themselves and have rituals and routines that help them to keep up healthy habits even when traumatic or difficult things happen. Others might not have been lucky enough to grow up in an environment where healthy sleep habits, good food and routines for self-care were taught, practised or modelled by the adults around them. Even when you've been lucky and grown up with good healthy routines and habits, a traumatic event can throw you off course completely. Brushing your teeth and eating a healthy breakfast just don't feel like priorities or something worth doing. Having a short period of 'going to ground' or hiding under the covers can be helpful and healthy to let us process, adjust and rest following a difficult experience. If this lack of routine and care for yourself goes on for more than a few days and runs into weeks, however, it can have a bad effect on your mental health and recovery from the trauma.

Often young people feel irritated when psychologists like Bridie and Sue talk to them about sleep, food, exercise and breathing. When you've been through a really tough time these can feel unimportant, but they really are crucial to getting back on track and feeling like yourself again. If this has been a lifelong pattern of struggling with self-care, it might be tougher to establish these things, but it's still just as important for your mental health and recovery moving forward.

We hope that these ideas get you started on the right path. Many of them lead into other chapters and will be helped by ideas later in the book, but making small changes to your habits and routines early on can be helpful later down the line. So, in summary, these things may feel small, but they make a big difference.

Keep doing (or start doing) things that make you feel good – play is healing and not just for little children

Sometimes if we've witnessed or been part of a traumatic event or been in an environment where others didn't care for us and make us feel safe and important, then it can feel as if we don't deserve to enjoy life, or do or have nice things. Our trauma can trick us into thinking that we feel so bad because we're bad and somehow to blame or 'not strong enough' to have stopped bad things from happening. Even little children who have very little physical capability to stop adults or to even get away from danger can feel this great sense of responsibility. Guilt and shame are very common but are a huge block to recovery and developing healthy coping and a positive sense of yourself as you grow and become an adult.

We want you to know that you're not dishonouring people who have suffered or are no longer here with you by doing enjoyable things and being playful or silly. You're creating a life worth living, and no matter what we've been born into or what terrible things we've seen or experienced, we all deserve this. We can honour those we've loved and lost by being fully alive and present in the world. We can also make it clear to those that have hurt us or let us down that they didn't take away our ability to live a meaningful and happy life.

Positive activities

Make a big list of all the things that you've done or like to do that make you smile. It can be as small as 'calling my favourite aunt' or 'painting a picture' to 'going on holiday to Cornwall'. Once our threat system is activated and we feel unsafe, it can be hard to think of things that we can do, so having a list with lots of categories of activity, to help you pick the right one for how you're feeling, can help you to feel okay again. Jake's positive activities include: 'Watching YouTube, playing with fidget toys, having a little sleep, or playing with my dogs.'

You might use the four headings 'I want to feel...safe/calm/ connected/energized' and try to think of at least five things you can put under each heading. We hope you will pick up lots of ideas and how to action them as you're reading through this book. But to get you started, here are some examples.

Safe

1. Snuggle up under a soft blanket with a pet or soft toy.

2. Watch your favourite feel-good movie in bed.

3. Sit downstairs with someone you trust or ask them to come into your room.

4. Close your eyes and imagine your safe place, describing all the sights, sounds, smells, textures and tastes (see Chapter 6 for safety place imagery).

5. Light an incense burner and hum gently to yourself.

Calm

1. Repeat the mantra: 'Every day in every way this is feeling easier and easier.'

2. Use a breathing exercise or guided mindfulness exercise.

3. Do yoga movements to ground and calm yourself (see Chapter 7 for some ideas).

4. Give yourself a butterfly hug while tapping your shoulders.

5. Have a long bubble bath.

Connected

1. Call someone who makes you laugh.

2. Send a letter/email/postcard to someone who lives far away.

3. Ask someone to watch a movie with you snuggled up under a blanket.

4. Plan an activity to do with a friend (even just a walk).

5. Play your favourite game or sport with another person.

Energized

1. Do five jumping jacks.

2. Go for a brisk walk outside (even if it's raining!).

3. Sing along to your favourite song (really loud).

4. Try a new dance routine.

5. Play a physical game like tennis or swingball.

Breathing

Yes, we're going to talk to you about breathing, but please bear with us for a few more lines! What we know is that when people are feeling stressed, they tend to breathe in a far shallower way, gasp and briefly stop breathing or hyperventilate. So, if you can learn how to be more in control of your breathing at times when you're feeling stressed, this can help your body to feel okay and calmer again.

We don't advise constantly thinking about your breathing as it can be a trigger for some bodily responses that might relate closely to trauma. However, just being aware of your breaths and sitting or standing in an open posture and allowing your breath to enter and leave your body smoothly, and knowing that you need to breathe long and slow when you notice signs that you're feeling a threat response or any stress, is a good start for feeling calmer and more in control.

There are some very simple breathing techniques that can help to calm down your threat response. When we breathe out, we calm our threat system, lower our heart rate and counter the stress response. So, it can be helpful just to notice your breathing and try to make your out-breaths a little longer and deeper to help lower those physical signs of stress and tell your body that you're safe. Simply counting in for 7 and out for 11 can be enough (this is imaginatively called 7–11 breathing – you're welcome). Sometimes people make an audible sigh on the out-breath or choose a word to say on the out-breath (e.g. breathe, calm or relax) to prompt them to naturally make it longer.

Another example is bubble breathing. If you feel comfortable, close your eyes, or gently rest your focus on a space in the room. Put one hand on your chest, and one on your stomach (to make sure that you are breathing from your stomach area, which means that you are breathing deeply). Feel your chest rise on the in-breath and fall on the out-breath. Take slow breaths. Breathe in through your nose, then hold your breath for a count of five. Then breathe out through your mouth slowly, as if you were blowing a big bubble. Make sure that your out-breaths are longer than your in-breaths.

It can be nice to use a wand and bubble solution to do this. You might want to control your breathing and slow it down to blow big bubbles – see how big you can make them. You might want to blow lots of tiny bubbles. You then might want to catch some of the bubbles on your wand. It can be worth trying out lots of different types of bubble solution to find the ones that work best for you.

You could also use a guided breathing app to talk you through what to do, so you don't even have to really think about what you're doing at the time.

Getting a good night's sleep

Sleep is so, so important for helping you to recover from trauma and is often something that can be disrupted by bad dreams and worries. Or it might be that your traumatic experience happened at night-time, which might mean that your threat response is triggered at night and primed and ready to keep you safe (the opposite of the rest and relaxation that are needed for good sleep). It can feel as if sleep is not important because staying safe and alert is your priority. We need to change this to help you have better days and feel more able to manage some of the intense emotions and physical responses that can come after a traumatic experience.

If you're scared to go to sleep because of bad dreams or nightmares, see Chapter 9 where we talk about some ways to help with this. We know that nightmares can be terrifying and distressing. They can feel very real and make us feel powerless, and it's common for even adults to be scared to go to sleep. But we would recommend that even while you're finding the things that work for you with bad dreams, thinking about good sleep tips (or 'sleep hygiene' as it's often called) can be a helpful and important first step, preventing you from getting into a vicious cycle of over-tiredness that can actually trigger more stress reactions and make nightmares more likely. Keep reading and see if there are some things that you can do alongside strategies to help with the scary dreams.

Why is sleep important?

Although sleep might seem like a time when your body is relaxed and slowed down, or even switched off, this is definitely not the case. During sleep, your body is highly active, doing things that are important for your body and mind to function properly. Lots of physical things happen when we sleep, including our muscles recovering from all their use during the day and some important hormones (like growth hormone) being produced; sleep even helps us to grow. Importantly, it also helps us to process our emotions from the day, so a lack of sleep can lead to struggling with feelings. If sleep is not great or gets interrupted, we often feel more on edge, anxious or giddy. It seems as if the brain knows that we're lacking in energy, so it gives us a rush of feelings, helping us to keep going.

Sleep also helps us to use our mind effectively – without it, we can struggle to concentrate during the day, we might forget things, feel disoriented or even confused, making it hard to think clearly. Research has suggested that sleep is essential for our brain to naturally reset, which helps us to remember things and learn. Without a good night's sleep, we can therefore struggle physically, emotionally and mentally. So, this is one area of wellbeing in which you can take some positive steps, now you have this knowledge.

What's the right amount of sleep?

The amount of sleep needed for a healthy life changes as you grow older. Also, everyone is a bit different. Some people might be typically longer sleepers and some shorter sleepers. However, the average sleep 'requirements' are as follows:

- Age 5–13 years – approximately 9–11 hours per night

- Age 13–18 years – approximately 8–10 hours per night

- Age 18 and older – approximately 7–9 hours per night, but this gets a bit less in later life.

Your sleeping patterns

First, let's think a bit more about your sleep and where you might get stuck. If you understand more about your own sleeping patterns, such as the quality as well as quantity of your sleep, it can help you to think about what might improve it. It might also be useful to show your answers to someone close to you, to see if they can identify where you might be struggling.

Most nights...

What time do you start your bedtime routine (e.g. putting pyjamas on, brushing teeth)?

What do you do between your bedtime routine and sleep (e.g. check phone, watch TV)?

What time do you usually go to bed?

How long is it generally before you go to sleep?

How many times do you wake up in the night?

How long are you usually awake for?

What do you do when you wake up?

How much sleep, in total, do you get on an average night?

How many nights of the week do you struggle with your sleep?

How would you describe your sleep?

Do you feel refreshed after a night's sleep or still tired?

During the day...

Do you still feel tired?

Do you struggle to concentrate?

Do you feel moody?

What impact do your sleeping patterns have on your life?

What would be better if you could sleep more?

What have you already tried to get a better night's sleep?

What makes it more difficult to sleep?

Four ways to get a good night's sleep

This section gives you five different ways to improve your sleep, including thinking about the environment that you sleep in, how to improve your bedtime routine, helping your body and mind to relax, avoiding things that are likely to keep you awake, and minimizing distractions. Perhaps try out some of these and see which ones work for you.

1. Make your bedroom a sleep sanctuary

We talk more about making a room into a soothing safe place in Chapter 6. If your safe soothing place is your bedroom, then this can be helpful for improving sleep too. The place that you're sleeping in can have a massive impact on your ability to get to sleep and your quality of sleep. Some people can sleep pretty much anywhere, such as on a noisy train, but other people will struggle much more and might need a place where they can relax their body into a comfortable position, with limited distractions and stimulation (we mostly mean noise or light).

To help you feel comfortable, try to get the temperature right so that you're not too hot or cold. A cooler room with enough blankets to stay warm is generally best. A room that is too hot or one that is too cold can mean you feel restless and wake up more often. Opening the window for a little while before going to sleep can help to get the air in the room moving and make the room feel less stuffy.

Make the room dark and quiet. Some people like to just make their room completely silent (e.g. closing the door, removing noisy items). If you aren't lucky enough to have your own room then you can wear ear plugs to block out noises that might disturb sleep. Other people like listening to relaxing music or sounds as they're drifting off. Too much light in the room can make it difficult to fall asleep. You could use a sleep mask or blackout blinds to keep the light out.

2. Get a good routine

One of the best ways of training your body to sleep well is to get into a routine and to go to bed and get up at more or less the same time every day. This gets your body used to the pattern, so it's ready for sleep when you go to bed. Although it can be really tempting to take a nap during the day, particularly if you've not slept much the night before, it's best not to unless it's less than 20 minutes in the morning. If you take long naps later in the day, this just messes up your sleeping patterns at night, making you feel not sleepy and so not wanting to go to bed. Even if you had a bad night's sleep and are feeling super tired, try your best to keep your daytime activities the same as you had planned.

It's also better to only try to sleep when you actually feel tired or sleepy, rather than spending too much time awake in bed. If you haven't been able to get to sleep after about 20 minutes, get up and do something calming or boring until you feel sleepy (or read for a bit in bed), then get back into bed and try again (but if you can't fall asleep after another 20 minutes, then get up again... and keep going).

You can find your own sleep rituals to try to remind your body that it's time to sleep – some people find it helps to do relaxation stretches or breathing exercises or have a cup of non-caffeinated tea or warm milk.

3. Things to avoid

When we want to relax our body and mind, we need to slow down our thinking and calm the feelings in our bodies. Some of the things that we eat, drink and breathe will be unhelpful and make us feel more awake, alert and even hyperactive. These include caffeine, cigarettes and alcohol. So, it's best to avoid these for at least four hours (if not more) before going to bed. Energy drinks should also be totally avoided, as although they may make you feel less tired at the time, they will stop you from being able to get to sleep later. If you dance or do exercise in the evenings, it's best to do this as early as possible so that you've time to relax your mind and body before going to bed. Some people really enjoy having a small supper before going to bed (mmm, toast!) and this can actually be helpful for sleep. However, it's usually best not to have a big meal later on – small snacks are better.

4. Minimize distractions

In order to relax your mind, it helps to attempt to shut off from everyday distractions and demands. We can train our minds to get ready for sleep by following a good sleep routine (see 2 above), but sometimes this can be difficult if we're distracted by other things which can take up our focus and attention. Wherever possible, try not to use your bed for anything other than sleeping, so that your body starts to associate your bed with sleep. If you use your bed as a place to watch TV, eat or work on your laptop, then your body will not learn the bed–sleep connection as well.

One of the biggest things that stops most people (including us) from sleeping is looking at our phones. It can be so tempting to just check something on the internet or see why it beeped, but this will bring your mind straight out of your sleep routine and back into being active. Even worse than this, recent research has told us that time looking at screens (such as your phone) can cause sleep problems, like poorer quality sleep and taking longer to fall asleep. There's a biological reason for this, as there's a blue light which shines out of your phone (and other devices) which prevents a sleep hormone called melatonin from being released. The level of this hormone usually increases a few hours before you go to sleep and is like a signal to the body to prepare you for sleep. So, when this hormone isn't released, it will be far more difficult for you to fall asleep. Also, the lights behind the screens of devices can cause the brain to be more alert (tricking the brain into thinking that it's daytime), getting in the way of a good night's sleep even more. Although lots of us may end up going on our phones and looking through our social media accounts, this is likely to delay and interrupt our sleep routines. It will keep our minds busy and active and we might get drawn into a conversation or worry. We often suggest to young people and their family that they have an agreement where they plug the phone in downstairs at 8pm for the night so that it can't be getting in the way of a good night's sleep.

Another big distraction that people often talk about is watching the time. When you're struggling to sleep, it can be easy to keep checking the time to see how long it is since you last checked and how long until the morning. However, checking the time during the night is likely to reinforce unhelpful thoughts such as 'It's so late, I can't sleep' or 'I've only slept for four hours'. These thoughts can make you feel anxious or frustrated, meaning you are less likely to fall asleep. It can also have an even worse effect if you check the time on your phone (see above information about the screens of devices). So, try to check the time less and only when you really need to.

Eating well

As well as getting a good night's sleep, it's important to make sure that you're eating a balanced diet with lots of fresh fruit and vegetables. This might seem like another eye-rolling nag to have at someone when they've been through trauma/s, but when your body and mind think there's a threat, it can change your appetite and you can misunderstand some of the feelings in your body. You might simply forget about healthy eating and crave more carbohydrates and sugar to try and soothe your feelings. Because your stomach feels strange from the lack of blood flowing to it, you might stop eating at regular mealtimes as you just feel sick and yuck and think your body is telling you not to eat. This is a problem because your body's responses to over- or under-eating, or eating the wrong things, can then interact with your stress and threat response and make you feel even worse. If you're not eating regularly, or not eating the right foods, then sudden surges and drops in your blood sugar can mean you don't feel okay in your body at all. You can lack energy or feel a bit giddy or cycle between the two. Trying to make sure that you're eating healthy food at mealtimes, with regular nutritious snacks, is a good starting point for feeling okay and being able to cope when life throws you some stress and triggers big feelings.

Eating is also highly social. We often eat with our family, friends or the important people we live, work and study with. When we remove regular meals from our day, we also miss opportunities to connect with these people and can feel more isolated and alone with our experiences and how we're feeling.

Exercise

There's now a lot of research and a growing understanding that being active is vital to psychological wellbeing and recovering from trauma. We talk a lot more about this in Chapter 8, especially how sport can help us to heal from trauma. When we say exercise, we don't always mean going to the gym for a full workout. Activity that improves your mood and mental health can range from walking more steps each day, to running marathons. Things that might get you inspired and move your focus on from difficult experiences can include boxing, rock climbing, joining a sports team or wild swimming in the (often freezing) outdoors.

So how does it help? Well, exercise releases lots of chemicals in the brain that we know are associated with feeling good in our bodies and with a sense of 'wellbeing'. These chemicals are things that can get out of balance when people face traumatic experiences. Exercise gets the good chemicals going. Exercise is known to improve sleep (see section above) and to boost energy levels throughout the day. Physical activity and the way it makes you feel can then be a coping strategy that you use instead of harmful things like eating junk food or drinking alcohol that actually make you feel worse in the long run. As well as the chemicals, there's often a sense of mastery and achievement (I ran further/faster, or climbed higher, learned a difficult dance routine), and this boosts your mood and resilience further.

Start small and try to include others in your plans. Ask a friend to join you for a walk. Go swimming with someone you trust. If you're struggling to feel safe when you're out and about then try some of the beginner's yoga on YouTube on your bedroom floor and try to do ten minutes every day, then give yourself a nice reward afterwards. Put some music on at home and dance! Any kind of movement is good and every little bit will help.

Drugs and alcohol: trauma and addiction

Alcohol has long been a socially acceptable way for adults to manage their feelings and stress when life throws difficult or traumatic experiences their way. Think about how in England historically you might have been offered brandy after a terrible shock or trauma. Professionals often talk about 'self-medicating' and often see addiction not as the problem, but a symptom or more likely a coping strategy. We use substances to help us to feel okay again when our body feels strange and unpleasant, and we're overwhelmed by our emotions. Some people may use a substance to stop their mind racing and their body feeling tense, or they may use something else that makes them feel 'buzzed' and confident if they suddenly feel scared and unable to talk to others.

Although adolescence is a time of experimentation and risk-taking, it feels important to say that substances can be helpful in making you feel better in the short term and helping you to forget or feel less impacted by your experiences, but sadly the long-term impact of this can make it impossible for you to actually deal with the trauma you've experienced. It may prevent you from finding healthy and helpful ways to deal with your difficult feelings and memories. Substances can take over and be your only way to respond and manage your emotions and traumatic memories, making it harder to motivate yourself to work on the positive routines and activities that can help you to connect to others and feel safe again. See Appendix IV for some information about a helpline and website where you can access information and support around drug and alcohol use.

◊ Chapter 6 ◊

Managing Intense Emotions

Trauma and difficult life events can cause intense or overwhelming emotions, which can feel difficult to manage and cope with. As we've explored in previous chapters, when our threat system is activated, it can bring up emotions like anger, distress, fear and even terror. So, in this chapter, we'll explore ways to 'soothe the threat system' using skills from dialectical behaviour therapy (DBT) and compassion-focused therapy (CFT), and everyday tips from young people.

It helps when we can practise feeling soothed, as this is like building a muscle. When we practise and train ourselves in soothing, it becomes much quicker and easier to feel soothed again. So please do have a go at some of these strategies when you're feeling okay too, or even better, build them into your everyday routine.

Unintended consequences

Sometimes when we experience intense emotions, and feel overwhelmed by them, we'll try to get rid of them however we can. Quick fixes such as overworking, taking drugs, drinking alcohol or hurting ourselves can distract or block these out at first. The problem is that although we might feel okay or better for a short period of time, there are unintended consequences that can make us feel worse in the longer term, such as ending up feeling exhausted, not sleeping, doing something illegal or harmful to our bodies, or not really dealing with what's happening underneath (leading to longer-term problems).

Are there any things that you might do as a way of feeling soothed that don't feel that helpful in the end, or that you end up feeling bad about afterwards?

In this chapter, we'll explore a range of more healthy and helpful strategies that can help you to activate your soothing system and calm your threat system.

Safeness and soothing system

In compassion-focused therapy (CFT), we talk about the safeness or soothing emotional regulation system. When we feel soothed, this system releases chemicals in our bodies called endorphins (and also oxytocin when we're being soothed by other people) which can help us to feel at peace, calm and content, safe and at ease. Any difficult threat-based emotions that we might have been feeling are quickly soothed.

As we're social beings, we crave connection with others. When we experience soothing from other people who we feel comfortable and safe around, this can lead us to feel connected to them and can activate our soothing system. People whom we trust and feel close to sometimes soothe us by just being physically close, listening to us and trying to understand how we're feeling. Sometimes, just by being near someone else who is calm and relaxed can help us to feel calm and more relaxed too (we can 'catch' their calmness). We might also want physical closeness and touch from others, such as someone holding our hand, giving us a big hug, stroking our hair, or rubbing our back or feet. It all depends on what you feel comfortable with, and what's soothing and comforting to you.

It can be helpful to think about all the important people in your life, and consider which of these relationships help you to feel safe, calm and connected. Also, which of these people and relationships lead you to feel unsafe, on edge and disconnected? Or lead to you feeling intense emotions?

As we discussed in Chapter 4, sometimes you might have learned protective strategies in your relationships to keep you safe from others. However, these might lead you to push people (including those closest to you) away. Where someone is safe, it can be useful to try to let your protective barriers down and allow yourself to access their support.

Ask yourself:

– Who helps me to feel safe, calm and soothed?

– Are there any people in my life who I would like to get to know more, or spend more time with?

– Which activities do I enjoy doing with others that help me to feel close to them, calm and soothed?

Playing and having fun with other people, and laughing together, is also a good way of building a closer connection. Where you have fun with someone else, your threat system 'goes offline', and your ability to connect increases. You might feel as if you're getting too old to play, but Bridie and Sue still like to play, and if they're not too old...

So, we really encourage you to think about games and silly things that you might like to do with your friends and family to get you playing and laughing.

A FEW IDEAS FOR PLAYFULNESS

◇ Uno or other card games

◇ Team sports like football

◇ Something crafty and messy

◇ Trampolining

◇ A water fight

◇ Board games or games like Klask and Yes!/No! Game

◇ Roller skating

◇ Dancing and cartwheeling

'Name it to tame it'

This might sound like a really simple strategy (and it is!), but it's actually one of the most effective. The phrase 'name it to tame it' comes from a clinical professor of psychiatry called Dan Siegel. Dan found that one of the main things that helps us to be able to calm our emotions is the ability to recognize and name our emotions as we experience them.

Often the intensity of our emotions might feel even worse when we've experienced trauma, as our emotions might feel really over-whelming and all muddled up. Or it might be that we've never really been good at telling our emotions apart.

But also, it's really important *how* we talk about our emotions. Sometimes there's a danger that we talk about our emotions as if we are our emotions. For example, someone might say 'I'm sad' or 'I'm worried'. What Dan found is that this can make the emotions feel stuck and hard to change. However, if we talk about emotions as something that we're experiencing, and something external to us, this can make them feel more changeable and as if we're more in control of them; for example, 'I *feel* sad' or 'I *feel* worried'.

It might also be that we don't have the words to say how we're feeling. Here are some of the common feelings that people might have when they have been through difficult experiences or trauma. Have a look to see if any of these fit your experience, but you might want to add your own in too.

I feel unsafe/powerless/helpless/hopeless/trapped/vulnerable.

I feel awkward/uncomfortable/jittery/hyper/silly.

I feel unloved/uncared for/alone/lonely/isolated/abandoned/rejected/ignored.

I feel worthless/unimportant/unheard/ignored/not good enough/insignificant.

I feel scared/terrified/worried/afraid/threatened/hesitant/nervous/stressed/cautious.

I feel angry/frustrated/irritated/resentful/annoyed.

I feel disgusted/repulsed.

I feel jumpy/on edge/nervous/jittery.

I feel blamed/ashamed/bad/guilty/embarrassed/humiliated.

I feel loss/sadness/grief/upset/discouraged/disappointed/empty/hurt/full of pain.

I feel overwhelmed/like everything is too much/muddled/confused.

I feel powerful/in control.

I feel nothing/empty/disconnected/zoned out/cut off/dazed.

It can be useful to check-in with yourself on a regular basis and try to name how you feel. You might feel a range of emotions, or just one emotion strongly, or you might feel that you're not experiencing any emotions at all. Just naming the emotions that you feel can help you to start to feel more in control of them. Where possible, it can be helpful to talk through these emotions with a trusted adult – not for them to do anything as such, but just to listen.

Sometimes, it can also help to write down how you're feeling, such as in a diary or even on a piece of paper or post-it that you might throw away. Whatever works for you. You might also find it helpful to draw out the emotions that you feel.

RIDING THE WAVES OF EMOTIONS

When you've worked out how you're feeling, it can be useful to think about what kind of things might help you to get through, tolerate or 'ride the waves' of the emotion.

The next few sections will outline some strategies that young people have found helpful in getting through intense emotions, especially those linked to trauma.

Glitter bottle – mixed-up emotions

Sometimes it can be really hard not to just respond to our emotions but instead give ourselves the time to calm and soothe.

Lots of people like making a glitter bottle as a way of pausing and giving time before reacting. To do this, get as many colours of glitter as you can and then think about the different emotions that you experience. Name each colour a different feeling; for example, you might name them 'fearful', 'confused', 'angry' and 'unsure'. Then pour all the glitter into a plastic bottle that has a screw top lid. Add some water and a little drop of PVA glue. Now this is your glitter bottle full of emotions. When you start to feel all mixed up, you can shake the bottle. Watching the glitter settle can be a visually soothing experience, but there is also a second important way you can use it. When you're feeling all mixed up, this isn't a great time to make decisions or respond to others. So, instead, use this time to watch the glitter and do some deep breaths (or another coping strategy). Don't do anything else until your feelings (the glitter) have settled.

Warm your face

Start by rubbing the palms of your hands together for a few seconds until they start to feel warm, then gently cover your eyes with your palms. Place your fingers on your forehead, and your palms over your eyes but not touching them. Just spend a minute or two enjoying the warmth and peace.

Muscle relaxation

As discussed in Chapters 2, 7 and 8, when we experience trauma reactions or intense emotions, we often start to hold tension in our body. So, it can be useful to help our body to 'let go' of this tension so that we can feel relaxed again. Doing this can help us to know that we can control how tense our muscles feel, so we can use these strategies at times that we need them.

The first, and perhaps easiest, strategy is to just notice any tension in your body and try to let go of it. For example, Sue always notices that she holds tension in her shoulders (sometimes they're so tense that they're moving up towards her ears). If she notices this, she then tries to let it go and relax her shoulders while taking a deep breath. This immediately helps her to feel a little better. Sometimes this is known as the 'uncooked noodle' strategy, as what you're really trying to do is relax your body so that rather than being stiff and rigid like an uncooked noodle, it starts to relax bit by bit like a noodle does as it cooks.

Another one of the strategies that we can use is called 'progressive muscle relaxation'. The idea of this is that if we tense our muscles tightly first, and then let go, it can lead to a deeper state of relaxation than if we had simply just attempted to let go and relax. To do this, you might want to lie or sit down. Then start with your toes, then feet, and squeeze tightly for a few seconds (perhaps for a count of five), then release. Then move on to your legs, squeeze the muscles tightly, hold for a few seconds, then release. Slowly work your way up your body, squeezing then releasing your muscles until your body moves into a more relaxed state.

Alternatively, having a hot bath (with bubble bath or bath salts – whichever you prefer) can be relaxing. Or you might prefer doing some gentle stretches or yoga. Massage can also be a nice way to relax muscles, and touch in itself can be really soothing. You could go for a massage, use a massager, or massage your own hands, legs or feet.

Safe place imagery

Using imagery (imagining safe people or places in our minds) can be a helpful strategy, which can bring feelings of safeness and calmness. At times when we're feeling unsafe or scared, we can then go away in our minds to this safe place to help us to feel okay again. In fact, safe place imagery is used a lot during trauma therapy, so that people can access a safe place in their minds if their memories are becoming too scary or distressing. Safe place imagery can be especially useful when our traumatic experiences included feelings of physical threat or fear.

The first step is to start to think about a place (real or imaginary) which helps you to feel safe, calm and soothed. The place could be anywhere, but if it's a real place, make sure that there are no difficult memories linked to it (as if there are, these could be brought up by the exercise). You can be as creative as you want. You might choose a big field, lying on your back on the soft grass, with the sun on your face, watching the clouds pass slowly in the sky. Or you might choose paddling in the sea, or baking in a massive kitchen, or wandering around a castle, or sitting next to a roaring fire. Whatever feels most soothing and comforting to you.

- What would your safe place be like?

- What would you see there? Would it be outside or inside?

- Would it be warm or cold?

Play about with these questions, and try to stay curious with yourself, asking yourself whether these things would help you to feel safe and comforted, or whether you would prefer something a little different. Perhaps imagine that you're an artist making a new masterpiece just for yourself, trying new things out and seeing what works and how each brushstroke makes you feel and whether you want to keep it like that or try something different again.

When you feel that you've developed an initial idea of a safe place, work through your senses one by one and imagine what detail they will add to your safe place. It can help to close your eyes and imagine that you've walked into your safe place, and then look around and explore it a little, allowing your mind to be creative while still staying with feelings of safeness and calmness. The more details that you can work out, the better your imagery will be (although these details may change over time, as your safe place can change, as long as the feelings of safeness and calmness remain).

Here are some questions about your safe place to consider:

– Look around you – what can you see?

– What colours are around you? Are they dark or light?

– If you're outside, where are you? What does the sky look like above you?

– Is there someone else with you (person or animal), or are you by yourself? If there's someone with you, who is it that makes you feel safe and soothed?

– What are you doing and what can you physically feel?

– Are you lying down, walking or sitting down? What does it feel like?

– Are you feeling warm or cold?

– Now think of any other sensations that you might have in your safe place such as a gentle cooling breeze, or the warmth of the sun on your face. What can you hear, either close to you or far away?

– What kind of smells or tastes are associated with your safe place – ones that help you to feel safe, calm and soothed?

– Which emotions do you feel when you're in your safe place?

If you struggle to do this by yourself, you might want to get an audio-guided safe place imagery exercise to help you to think things through with your eyes closed. Guided imagery exercises such as 'Safe Place' are often available through relaxation apps or can be downloaded from the internet (e.g. www.compassion atemind.co.uk/resource/audio). You also might want to build a collage of pictures that you might associate with your safe place, to help you to strengthen it and really think it through.

If you were to choose one word that you would associate with your safe place, what would it be? We can call this a cueing word, as it can be a word that we can start to use when thinking about our safe place, but then if we use it enough, it can also be a word that when we think of it, it brings feelings of safeness and calmness at other times too.

It can be useful to practise and deepen your safe place imagery on a regular basis, ideally each day. The more that you practise and build on this, the stronger the imagery will be when you need it.

Cueing word or smell

As we've said above, a cueing word can be a good way to trigger feelings of calmness and safeness. If we repeatedly associate a word with feeling calm or safe (such as using it during a safe place imagery or other relaxation exercise), when we use the word again at another time, it can bring about a response in our mind and body of calmness and safety. For example, Sue's cueing phrase is 'Let go', as when she's feeling safe and calm it's as if her body and mind let go of any tension or stress. So, Sue will say the phrase 'Let go' to herself when she's doing any calming coping strategies. This means then that at other times when Sue needs to feel more relaxed, she can say 'Let go' to herself and it quickly brings on feelings of calmness, as it does when she's doing her coping strategies.

Another way to cue your mind to experience a relaxation response is through a soothing smell. Using your sense of smell can be a quick way of accessing an emotional response (both positive and negative), so you can use it to trigger your soothing system quickly and effectively. Are there any particular smells that are soothing and calming to you? There might be some smells that bring up a particular memory, such as a food smell that reminds you of childhood, or a perfume that reminds you of someone close to you. As we talked about in Chapter 2, when we're reminded of something through our sensory input, we often feel the emotions associated with that memory before we remember what the memory actually is. For example, we may feel warm and content when we smell something that reminds us of a food that we liked when we were younger.

So, you can train your soothing system to be associated with a particular smell that you like. This could be a perfume or aftershave, an essential oil, a bag of lavender, a particular strong-smelling sweet and so on. It can be useful to have a big sniff of the smell at the beginning, during and the end of every soothing exercise that you do. This then gives the best chance for your brain to start to associate the smell with the soothing feelings that you have during the exercise. When you've done this lots of times and your brain has started to make this link, then you can smell the scent whenever you need to, to trigger soothing and calm feelings.

Sensory soothing

A good, easy way of helping your body to feel soothed is through using your senses. You might get some ideas through the safe place exercise above as to what helps you feel safe and soothed, but otherwise, you can think through each sense and the different sights, smells, textures, sounds and tastes that help you to feel calm and soothed. We even sometimes think about the sixth sense of movement (which movements help you to feel soothed?) if you want to add this in too, and we'll talk about this more in the following chapters. Jake enjoys soothing techniques: 'Smile and hug someone to make you feel better, snuggle up in bed or on the couch and watch a film or YouTube, and relax and eat cake. It helps.'

IDEAS OF SENSORY SOOTHING ITEMS

Sight – glitter jar; pictures of places/people that help you to feel safe; watching a candle; soothing colours/maybe a colouring book; ASMR (autonomous sensory meridian response) videos; collage of soothing things; low lighting; sleep mask.

Sound – listening to calming music or noises (such as nature sounds); guided relaxation exercises; listening to someone's voice that you feel soothed by; gentle drumming/rhythm.

Smell – soothing food or hot drink; lavender or other essential oils; perfume or aftershave; bath or shower stuff; pillow spray; fresh air; candles or incense.

Touch – wrapping up in a blanket; wearing a big warm hoody, scarf or woolly hat; cold ice pack; hot bath or shower (or cold bath or shower – whatever's calming to you); popping bubble wrap; play doh or putty; baking and kneading; cuddling a soft toy or a person; holding someone's hand; having a massage; a weighted blanket.

Taste – hot chocolate or other hot drink; eating something crunchy or something with a nostalgic taste.

Have a think about what helps you personally to feel safe and soothed using the senses, then make sure that you've some of these items around when you need them. Even better, use these items regularly to have lots of sensory soothing breaks. Sometimes people like to create a self-soothe box or drawer, so that their sensory soothing items can be kept in one place for when they most need them.

Safety and soothing inside and outside our homes

In Denmark, there's one all-encompassing word for a lifestyle that brings positive wellbeing: 'hygge'. This describes a way of living that is cosy, caring, content, friendly and safe. It fits really well with the feelings of safety, comfort and calm that we've talked about so far in this chapter. So, one way to enhance this even more is to start to think about how to make your environment feel more comforting.

Look around your environment/room/house and notice which items bring you a sense of soothing and which items bring you a sense of unease. Look around your home and find the places that feel cosy, comforting and connecting, then identify what makes them feel that way. Notice the objects around you that bring up feelings of safety, contentment and warmth. Start to make small changes to your spaces to help you create 'safe spaces' for yourself where you can find peace and can go to when you need a bit of calmness and soothing. And yes, this is a really good excuse to buy a new fluffy blanket.

In addition to finding safe places indoors, we also know that being outside in nature can be really soothing and grounding; it can calm intense emotions and bring on feelings of relaxation. This can be something as simple as going for a walk, or even just looking at a picture of the outdoors (such as a mountain range, a beach or a forest).

One theory about the calming impact of nature talks about the blue and green effects. The green effect suggests that being in green spaces in nature can enhance our psychological and physical well-being. For example, we might go for a walk in a wood, stand on grass with bare feet, or bring plants or flowers into our homes. The blue effect suggests that being in or around water can enhance our psychological and physical wellbeing and reduce levels of stress.

This could just mean being close to water, such as going for a walk along a beach or next to a lake, or going for a paddle or swim.

Creating a toolkit – what works for you?

There are lots of different practical coping strategies that you can use, some of which we've already mentioned and some we'll talk about in the next few chapters, and there are lots of others out there too. Some common ones include going for a run or walk, having a bubble bath or hot/cold shower, doing something creative or something distracting (like a puzzle or board game), singing, dancing or playing music, playing a game on your phone, looking at funny videos, listening to music or a podcast through headphones (having a playlist set up with angry, calming or energetic music), and talking to someone safe. But everyone is different, so it's important to work out which strategies work best for you. Which strategies help you when you're feeling stressed, overwhelmed, distressed and fearful? Which help you to feel okay again? One way to work out what helps you personally is to try out different strategies and rate the intensity of your emotions before and after you've used each one to see which ones work best to calm your emotions. When you know which ones work for you, perhaps write these out somewhere so that you know what to do when you're feeling overwhelmed or distressed.

Chapter 7

Taking Control of Your Body

As we learned in Chapter 2, trauma affects both our mind and our body. Sometimes people even talk about how the trauma that we experienced is 'stored' in our body, and that when we experience threat again, we can sometimes feel the same, or similar, reactions.

As Rach explains:

> I was sceptical [about therapy], however the therapy helped me to process my trauma memories of a car accident years ago. When concentrating on the original experience, my muscles remembered what had happened to me, my right leg tingled and I felt discomfort in my lower back as if my body felt the memory of the incident, the muscle memory. This really surprised me and I found it really powerful to feel that not only was my brain processing the memories, in order to come to terms with and file away the experience, but my body was doing the same.

This chapter will therefore focus on how to take back control over trauma-based bodily reactions.

When we experience a trauma reaction, our body might prepare itself to move, which means that we suddenly feel full of energy and ready to react, and our muscles become tense. Usually this is to get us ready for fight or flight. But what about when this doesn't happen? The threat doesn't present itself, but our body is still full of energy and ready to move. This can lead to us feeling jittery, on edge or jumpy, and this can be a really horrible feeling to have, which can lead us to react in an exaggerated way to things (e.g. jump at something small). You might have heard adults or professionals talk about 'internal restlessness' where you may look still and calm but inside you feel all jumpy.

So, some of the strategies in this chapter will focus on helping you to get rid of that excess energy and tension and feel okay again.

Sometimes when we experience a trauma reaction, however, our body reacts in a different way. Instead of energizing us, it can lead us to feel shut down, zoned out or dissociated. When this happens, we need strategies that help us to feel connected with our surroundings and help us to move. So, we'll look at these types of strategies that energize us too.

When working through this chapter, think about how you can notice if your body is zoned out and struggling to connect, full of energy and unable to relax, or feeling just right. Then perhaps try out the relevant strategies, see which ones work for you, how they make your body feel and how they alter your bodily reactions.

Strategies to get rid of excess energy

The aim of these strategies is to get rid of the high energy in your body and help you to feel just right. The idea is to continue to do the exercise until you feel that you've 'gone over the peak' of the energy. If you are thinking about effort levels, these ones should be about 6/10 or 7/10, so that you can really feel it in your body, but you're not exhausted by it.

Shake it out

Shake out your body, one part at a time, relaxing each body part as you shake it. Start with your hands, loosen them up and shake them out. Then add your arms too. Keep shaking. Then try adding in your legs, one at a time. Then perhaps raise your arms while shaking them. Then, if you want to, perhaps jump on the spot while shaking out your body. Do this for a minute or two. Then when you stop, notice what your body feels like.

Wall press

Find a sturdy wall. Using the flat palms of your hands, push against the wall as hard as you can, as if you're trying to push it over, and hold for approximately eight to ten seconds. Take your excess energy and push it away and into the wall.

Chair pose

This yoga position is also known as 'fierce' pose. There are many explanations of how to do this correctly on the internet, and you end up looking as if you're sitting in an invisible chair. The key steps are to begin standing, then bend your knees slowly, sinking your hips backwards as if you're sitting on a chair. As you do this, reach your arms high, above your head. This can be a tricky pose to do, but it can help to get rid of the built-up energy in your leg muscles.

Palm push

Place your palms together in front of you. Push them against each other, then hold for eight to ten seconds. Try to push that energy and tension out through your palms.

Jumping jacks

Do some jumping jacks, jumping into an X shape, then back into a standing position. Do enough to make you feel that you're starting to use up your energy.

Forward fold

Doing a forward fold, either sitting or standing, can help to activate your parasympathetic (calming) nervous system. When you fold forwards, allow your spine to round at the top, and let your arms and head fall forwards. This pose will help to regulate your blood pressure. Make sure that you take your time getting back up, as it can make you feel a bit dizzy at first.

Sunshine breaths

Stand up with your legs hip-width apart and keep your knees soft. Gently cross your wrists (one in front of the other). As you inhale, bring both hands up the front of the body (imagine that you're pulling off a jumper). When your arms are stretched above you, open your arms, and slowly lower them down to your sides as you exhale, drawing out a big circle. Then repeat. As you lower your arms and exhale, imagine that you're letting go of any stress or tension.

There are also lots of strategies (e.g. exercise, sport) that we'll talk about in the next chapter that can also help you to get rid of excess energy. Try to find what works for you.

Strategies to help you to reconnect

When you're feeling shut down, frozen or zoned out, you will need to first get energized before you can get to the point of feeling just right. The first thing to do is to start to move a little and connect back with your environment. Choose whichever activities feel most instinctive and natural to you, especially when you're feeling zoned out and shut down.

Feeling zoned out can feel preferable to being in an energized mode because it may be less overwhelming. It's important to notice if you don't want to engage with things or connect with other people, as if this is the case it's likely that you're shut down rather than relaxed and calm. Here are some strategies that might be useful when you're in the shut-down mode.

Any little movement

If you feel really shut down, sometimes it might feel like a big effort to just move. So, anything to start to activate your body, such as wiggling a finger or your toes, or going for a small walk to get a glass of water, can be useful.

Moving your neck

Often when you're shut down, your neck muscles can become quite frozen and tense. So, it can help to gently turn your neck from side to side. Look one way – what can you see? Pause for a minute, then gently move your head back to centre. Then look the other way – what can you see? Pause for a minute, then back to centre.

Raising your arms

Stand up, with your feet apart a comfortable amount and your knees remaining soft. Bring your arms up to the sides and hold them in the air. Hold them up for a minute or two. This exercise should be about a 6/10 effort, so you might want to push it a bit further or bend your arms slightly if it feels too much.

Rocking

Sway gently from side to side. You can do this sitting down or standing up, whichever you prefer. Try to find your centre – where it feels that you're reaching a central position – and perhaps pause there for a minute. Make slight movements rather than big movements.

Balance board

Using a balance board can be a good way of making sure that you're activating all the different parts of your body, while trying to stop yourself falling over. It can be a good way of helping you to feel grounded too.

Going on a swing

Having a swing can be a way to regulate through calm, predictable movements. Just a little effort is needed, then you can experience the gentle rocking motion of the swing.

Juggling

This can be a useful strategy to help to bring you back into your body, especially if you're not particularly good at juggling. You can use lots of different things to juggle, such as soft balls or fruit.

Cross patterning

Stand up, with your feet slightly apart. Raise your arms in the air, then bring one hand down to touch the opposite knee (which you can raise). Then swap arms and knees. Do this as fast or slow as you wish to. If you feel yourself zoning out, try to alter the pace to make sure that you're still engaged in the activity.

Eye focus

This exercise focuses on your peripheral vision. Put your thumb directly in front of you, then lift it upwards, and then draw a circle as wide as you can. Without moving your head, try to follow your thumb with your eyes – swap thumbs if you wish to at any stage, or use both thumbs and draw a large circle. When your thumbs fall out of your vision, wiggle them and see if you can see them then.

Humming bee breath

Sit or stand as comfortable. Close your eyes if you wish to. Then with your lips gently closed, take a breath and then make a humming noise on the out-breath. When you've done this, take another in-breath, then make a humming noise on the out-breath again. It doesn't have to be tuneful (but can be if you want it to be – perhaps choose a favourite song). You can also do this hum with your fingers in your ears, or on your earlobes, which can cause a more intense sensation. Try to hum for a minute or two, then see how you feel. When you exhale, it slows your heart rate, so any exercises like humming, singing or playing a wind instrument (where your out-breath is longer than your in-breath) can be useful.

Sue recently had some bad news about a family member. She felt herself go into shut-down mode. She probably appeared calm to people around her, but actually she was quite shut off from the outside world – she didn't want to talk or engage with anyone. Probably the most helpful thing for her was that she realized that she was shut down, so she knew that she could do something about it. She started by wiggling her toes. Then when she felt a little better, she stood on her balance board for about five minutes, quietly, just focusing on staying balanced (although, she did fall a few times). When she came off the board, she felt a little more energized and engaged again.

Feeling and staying just right

Now that you've read through this chapter, perhaps make a note of a few strategies that you want to try out. Have a go, and see what they feel like to you, and how they alter the way your body feels.

◇ Chapter 8 ◇

Exercise, Rhythm and Sport

In this chapter, we'll consider some of the ways that exercise, rhythm and sport might help with trauma reactions, and then think about how to choose your activity.

How can exercise help?

We know that sport and exercise have a range of benefits for people who have experienced trauma or bad stuff happening. Here are some of the ways in which exercise might help you to be able to move on from trauma.

1. Help with a freeze response

If you're someone who tends to 'freeze' or 'shut down' in situations which feel like a trigger or threat for you, exercise can help you to overcome this. When we move, through doing exercise or sport, we're letting our body know that we're safe, the trauma has ended, and we do not need our freeze response anymore. So when we practise regularly doing exercise and sport, this can help to wake our body up a little, increase feelings of safety, and move again.

2. Increase feelings of self-control

When we feel stronger and more in control, this can make us feel less vulnerable. Bessel van der Kolk, who is a bit of an expert around the treatment of trauma, has explained that when we experience trauma, we may feel that we're helpless to control what happens to us and how our body will react. However, when we are able to build strength in our body, and take control back, we can start to realize that we can have an impact on what our body is able to do, and how it can protect us – and even that the body can do things that we might not have realized that it could do. So, it's thought that when we engage with our muscles, this can lead us to feel physically stronger and more able to deal with any potential threats that might arise. Research has suggested that resistance or strength-based exercises can significantly reduce the anxiety that people might experience. Some activities such as martial arts, or strength-based training, can give people a sense of power, confidence and control. Also, when using sport or exercise, it can be a good way of building up our 'self-regulation skills' (learning how to calm down our bodily reactions and emotions and not act on impulses as quickly), which can help us to feel more in control of our bodies.

3. Get rid of excess energy and stress hormones

When our fight/flight response is triggered, we get a sudden urge to move. But when we then don't experience a threat, and don't need to fight or run, this can lead to a build-up of energy and stress hormones in our body (which can make us feel jittery, on edge and rubbish). When we move and exercise, this can help us to use up some of the excess energy and hormones, which then makes us feel a lot better. When Reggie is anxious, he finds that when he tackles or he's pushing in the scrum during a rugby game, this pushes all his anxiety and worries out. Exercise can also lead us to experience a rush of endorphins, which are chemicals in the brain that make us feel good and positive, and give us a natural high.

4. Find your rhythm

Rhythm is something that is a big part of our lives, even before we're born. We hear our mother's heartbeat in the womb, which provides us with rhythmic vibrations, pressure and sound. So, when we experience rhythms of a similar pace (60–80 beats per minute), this feels calming, safe and soothing to us. As we get older, repetitive rhythm can become a way of helping us to feel better, more balanced in our mind and body, and regulated and calm. It calms down our traumatized threat or survival response. Luckily, lots of exercises and sport include some sort of rhythm and repetition, such as running, walking, swimming, cycling, hitting/ kicking a ball back and forth, drumming, trampolining, singing and dancing. Doing repetitive rhythmic activities is now a recommended part of treatment for trauma, due to how it can help your brain start to 'integrate' (help the different parts of the brain to talk to each other better) and regulate (help you to be better able to feel in control of your emotions), to help to reduce hyperarousal (jumpiness, overwhelm, feeling on edge). Reggie finds throwing a ball in the air rhythmically or doing keepy-uppies distracts him and calms him down.

5. Build confidence and mastery

Research has told us that people who have had difficult experiences in their early life, but also regularly played sport, are less likely to struggle with their mental health as adults. Physical activities and playing sport in teams can help people who have experienced trauma to feel more in control, learn to regulate or calm their emotions or behaviours, and build good relationships with other young people. Taking part in sport can help us to feel more confident in our ability to cope with difficult events that might come up in the future, as we may feel more in control of our emotions and body. Sport can also teach us to keep going despite feeling frustrated, or following a loss, especially when this happens as part of a team. Reggie finds a real sense of belonging from playing team sports.

When his teammates give him feedback on his performance and they then listen to his feedback on them, he feels he's a valuable member of the team. It can also help us to challenge ourselves, and improve self-determination, motivation and confidence.

REGGIE'S USE OF SPORT

When I get anxious, physically my body goes tense and I go red. I can get butterflies, can't think properly, get really forgetful and even lose my appetite. Emotionally I get angry, worried I'm going to fail and think people are going to bully and hurt me or take me away from Mum and Dad, or even that they will send me away. My thoughts race and get bigger like rolling a snowball. What helps is when I do sport, such as cricket, rugby and football. My worries and anxiety seem to shrink away because all I focus on is the ball and trying to get the ball or hit it and throw it as far as I can. Also, being part of a team makes me feel that I fit in somewhere and I'm needed and wanted.

Finding your activity

There are so many different exercises and sport that you could do. You might want something by yourself, or some sort of group sport which you can do with one other person or a group of people. The important thing is to find something that:

- you like and enjoy doing (where possible!), which will help you to carry on doing it

- you can easily access as and when you need it, or on a regular basis

- meets your needs. You might want to choose something that calms you, builds your strength, gets rid of excess energy, has a good rhythm, or that you just enjoy.

It's completely up to you! Here are some ideas (but there are lots more):

- Dancing

- Trampolining

- Drumming

- Strength-based training/weights

- Running or walking

- Martial arts

- Yoga or pilates

- Kicking a ball back and forth

- Football

- Rugby

- Cricket.

Sometimes, when people have experienced trauma, they might find more cardio-based exercise difficult at first. When their heart rate and breathing rate rise, this might trigger feelings of panic or overwhelm. Therefore, it can be easier to start with activities that are slower and more purposeful, which do not particularly increase heart or breathing rate.

So, what does this actually look like?

Terry Angus was a professional football player who has since worked with the youth justice system, the Connexions service, and as the Community Equalities Executive for the Professional Footballers' Association (PFA). As Terry has worked with, and supported, lots of young people who have had difficult experiences using exercise and sport, we thought that we would pick his brains about how this might help people to move on from trauma. Reggie and Sue interviewed Terry.

How do you think that sport might help young people to overcome or move on from trauma?
I'll talk from personal experience. When I've faced trauma, I've used sport and movement as a way not of forgetting but helping me through it. And by sport and movement, that might just be walking down the road; that might be getting engaged in high-level physical activity. But to be able to go out there and move around and use sport...it helped me come to terms with what I was doing, what I was thinking. The pain I suffered through trauma was all consuming... then going and being able to do sport...meant that some of that all-consuming pain, I had to shift...into doing the sport. Now, when I did the sport, it raised some of those endorphins within my body, which made me feel better. It made me go, 'Okay, so my trauma is still bad, but you know what, there's still a world outside the trauma. There's another hour, there's another tomorrow.' So it kind of helped me understand the trauma more, rather than sink further and further and further down into an abyss where I couldn't really get out... It's not just about playing. It might just be about watching, it might be about being involved in it, it might be a volunteering aspect, it might be playing, but sport has such a big impact on my life, in terms of helping me get through any sort of difficulties I had.

Now what I would always say is this. You might decide to go do some rock climbing in the Peak District. Great. But that's going to last for a day, half a day. And then tomorrow, what are you going to do? So, using sport as a mechanism for helping with trauma, it's got to be something that the individual can tap into whenever trauma starts to take over. Now if you're doing rock climbing, and trauma is taking over you at 7pm on a Tuesday evening, you can't just go out and do rock climbing, especially if you live in an inner city. So, it needs to be something that you can access yourself, and that you can find within an hour, or within that day when you might need it, whether that be cricket, rugby, running, walking, football, whatever.

Are there any types of exercise or sport that are particularly helpful for people experiencing trauma?

It's hard to say because every situation is individual... It might be that for someone the trauma is really emotional and high energy, so you might do boxing or football, which are both high energy too. But sometimes you might want to do the opposite and bring it right down instead, to something much calmer, like fishing or bowls... But, if a person deals with trauma by being reclusive and not coming out, you might want to do a high emotive sport instead, with a group interaction, like rugby or football. Even if a person enjoys football, it's important to find out if this is calming to them or likely to trigger them (such as missing a chance).

The benefit of group sport is that your mind is taken away from the trauma that you're suffering – you have to work as part of a team, think about other people and about their feelings. So that team effort helps because you've had no time to really think about your own personal trauma as you've had other things to think about. I've got to do this, I've got to run down the line, I've got to get the ball, I've got to give it to such and such, I've got to support this, that and the other... In individual sport, you have many more moments to actually think about what you've been going through.

You mentioned about sport being beneficial for your own wellbeing. Tell us more.

I don't drink, take drugs or smoke. For me, growing up, sport became that kind of release and enjoyment, so even now I will get up and go running every day, apart from Saturdays and Sundays. I'm not a great runner, but it's a release for me. Now a couple of times I've had a bit of an injury, and I haven't been able to run and that has been kind of difficult because the release for me hasn't been there... It's a habit now, it's vitally important. Being able to do those things has supported my wellbeing and has definitely helped with my bouts of dealing with trauma. So trauma comes, and I go to the crematorium, which is three, four miles from my house, and I may run there. Now I run there because I'm going to somewhere that causes me pain, but because I've run there, I feel better when I get there. And when I get there, the trauma is not as bad as if I had driven there. That's how I work.

◇ Chapter 9 ◇

Staying Grounded and Training Your Hippo

One of the biggest difficulties with trauma is that it can make our minds feel muddled and confused. Sometimes, the trauma reactions that we experience can feel so real, and as if the trauma is happening right now. So, our body reacts to what it *thinks* is happening (i.e. the traumatic event) rather than what's *actually* happening (i.e. sitting in our pyjamas watching Netflix).

So, one way of being a bit more in control of our trauma reactions is to learn to use grounding strategies. These are different types of strategies that aim to keep us 'grounded in the moment', focusing on what's *actually* happening, rather than what our body *thinks* is happening. We're all a bit different, so we tend to find that different people find different strategies helpful. It can be useful to try a few out and see which ones work for you, or even make your own.

The science-y bit

In our body, we've two different important sensory systems. Our external sensory system focuses on what's happening outside the body such as what we see, hear, smell, taste and touch. So, it gives us an idea of what's happening around us. Our internal sensory system is a bit different. It focuses on what's happening inside our body. This includes how we feel emotionally, what we can physically feel inside our body (e.g. butterflies in the stomach, heartbeat), our balance and spatial awareness. It tends to be best when we can have a bit of balance between these two systems, so that we're aware of what's happening around us, at the same time as being aware of how we're feeling inside.

When we're experiencing trauma reactions, sometimes this balance goes a bit off, and we can end up focusing more on what we're feeling inside our body and paying less attention to what's happening around us. We might notice that our body feels tense, and our breathing has quickened, so might think that this means there's a threat.

For example, a scary memory might pop into our mind. This might feel so real that our body becomes tense and we start to breathe quickly, as if we're panicking. This straightaway might make us feel that we're not safe, which makes us feel even more panicky and tense. So the more that we focus on our internal senses at these times, the worse we're likely to feel.

But what often we don't do when we're feeling so scared is to look around us to check out whether there is anything that we really need to be scared of right now. Or are we actually safe? So although we might feel that something is really unsafe (if we focus on how we feel inside), we might actually be quite safe (if we look around us instead).

TRY IT OUT...

One way to understand this a bit better is to have a go, at a time when you're in a safe place. Try walking around a room in your house. The first time that you walk round, focus on your external senses (what you can see, feel, smell, taste, touch). What did that feel like?

Then walk around the same room, but this time focus on your internal senses (what you feel in your body). What did that feel like?

Ideas for grounding strategies

When we use grounding strategies, we shift our attention away from our internal senses to our external senses, to 'break the cycle' and help us to feel safer, calmer and more in control. This can take a lot of practice at first, but it can mean we feel more in control of our trauma reactions. This chapter will give you some suggestions for grounding strategies that might help.

Naming

This is an exercise that you can do by yourself, or with someone else, and it makes you pay a lot of attention to what's happening around you.

Name:

- five things that you can see (e.g. chair, phone, book, carpet, window)

- five things that you can hear (e.g. clock ticking, sound of cars on the road, someone talking in the distance, dog barking, your breathing)

- five things that you can physically feel (e.g. your socks on your feet, your hair on your neck, the cool breeze, the chair you're sat in, your fluffy top on your skin).

When you've done this (you might have to take a few minutes to really notice these things), name four things that you can see, four things you can hear and four things that you physically feel. Then three, two and one...

Reminding yourself

It can help to tell yourself (either out loud or in your head) who you are now, how old you are, what year it is, where you are and what you're doing. This can help to ground yourself in the here and now (and remind yourself that you're not in the past). For example, 'I'm Ella. I'm 16, and it's January 2023. I'm in my room at home in Warrington, listening to music. I'm going to get lunch with my friend in a bit, and we're going to have sandwiches then cake.'

Body awareness

Chapter 7 talks a lot more about body awareness and how to use your body to make you feel okay again. But there are also a few ways of stretching and moving your body which can help to quickly ground you:

- Take a few long, deep breaths and feel your stomach rise and fall.

- Put your feet flat on the floor (ideally bare feet) and stamp them a few times, noticing how this feels.

- Where possible, walk barefoot on the ground or carpet.

- If you're lying or sitting down, notice the feeling of the hard floor underneath you.

- Press the palms of your hands together and hold them like this for ten seconds, then relax. Notice how this feels.

- Reach your arms up above your head and stretch as high as you can, for a few seconds, then relax.

Extreme sensations

One way to make sure that your mind is paying attention to your external senses is to use an extreme sensory item. This time you're not trying to soothe (as discussed in Chapter 6), instead you're trying to grab your attention with this sensory item. For example, eating a sweet that is super sour (e.g. sour Skittles), an extra, extra strong mint, or some food that is extremely spicy, or a really strong taste (like really salty, sour, salt and vinegar crisps). It can be very hard to focus on anything else when eating something like this!

Or you might, for example, have an icepack (or ice in a ziplock bag) that you can keep in your fridge or freezer, which you can hold against your face or chest if you're having a trauma reaction. This will 'grab' your attention onto your external senses (away from the internal ones). If you don't have access to this, holding a cold drink (can or bottle) to your face, or splashing your face with cold water, can also work. Or even eat an ice lolly or have a cold drink.

A really strong smell that you like (e.g. an essential oil, peppermint, or strong-smelling hand cream) could also work, as could some loud or happy music (depending on what you prefer), again to grab your attention.

Something that you can feel physically may also be useful. Sometimes people find weighted blankets very soothing (Sue has several in her therapy rooms), or things like slap bands, an elastic band or hair bobble round the wrist (which can be pulled on), or even a face mask or waxing legs (pain, but safe pain) can be helpful and grounding.

Grounding objects

A useful strategy to use 'on the go' can be to find a grounding object, something that reminds you of safe, calming memories, that you can carry round with you all the time. For example, Sue has previously used a keyring with a bell on it that she picked up while on holiday, and a pebble. You could also choose a piece of jewellery. The object can then be used to remind you that you're safe, and you can hold it in your hand and pay attention to what it looks like and what it feels like when you hold it.

Grounding people

Often it can be most helpful when we have people around us whom we trust and can help us to stay grounded. People often don't know what to do, or how to help, when someone is experiencing trauma reactions, so sometimes it can be helpful to let them know in advance what does and doesn't help for you.

Also, sometimes it's just about having someone around us whom we feel safe and comfortable with, or who can distract us. When Reggie is feeling overwhelmed, he likes to be around his dogs. Just stroking them and having the weight of them on his lap can make him feel safe and calm.

Strategies for flashbacks

As we learned in Chapter 2, a flashback is an intense, vivid memory which can feel very real when someone is experiencing it. The following strategies build on the ones above to find ways to let your brain and body know that it's *just* a memory, and *not* real, which is a quick way of ending the trauma reaction.

When people talk about their flashbacks, they can often get understandably confused, as they can think that they're experiencing the trauma again, rather than it just being a memory. One of the things that helps us to feel more in control of flashbacks is to call them what they actually are (a memory), as this gives them less power. So however intense, vivid or distressing it is, it's a *memory*, rather than an experience. The reason why this is important is because memories can't hurt you, and they aren't dangerous, however much they may feel this way at the time. The more we can tell ourselves this, the more in control we become.

So, this means that our self-talk about our flashbacks is really important, as it impacts on the way that we experience them. For example, when we talk about the flashbacks as if they're experiences that are happening now, this can make them feel worse and more overwhelming (and can activate our threat system). But, if we can talk about them as memories, this can help to lessen their impact as we're reminding ourselves that they happened in the past and aren't happening now.

Here are some ways to do this:

- Write down a statement that you can keep with you and can repeat when you need it, that 'Flashbacks are just vivid memories, the trauma has ended', or something similar.

- When talking to yourself (either out loud or in your head), make sure that you change it to the past tense when talking about your flashbacks. You can also ask other trusted people to help you to do this. For example:

Flashback thinking	Remembering it's in the past
I'm going to die.	I felt as if I was going to die, but I survived.
I can hear screaming.	At the time, people were scared, and I remember that lots of people screamed.
They're grabbing me.	I was attacked.
I'm not safe.	I didn't feel safe, but I'm safe now.
It's all happening again.	I'm having a flashback, which is a vivid memory.

Using our external senses

As we talked about earlier in this chapter, we have both internal and external sensory systems. Usually, we use our internal senses to know what's happening inside our body and how we feel (e.g. I'm feeling worried, I'm hungry, my heart is beating fast), and our external senses to know what's happening around us. Usually it's our external senses that help us to know whether we're safe, and if there's anything in our environment that could potentially be a threat to us. But, sometimes, especially when we're having trauma reactions like flashbacks, we might swap, and actually look to our internal senses to figure out if we're safe or not. So, if our body feels tense, or our heart is beating faster, we might use this to decide that we're not safe at all (despite what's happening around us).

When we're experiencing a flashback, we tend to feel unsafe. Our internal senses are telling us that something is seriously wrong (because of all of the bodily reactions that we're experiencing, based on the flashback that we're having), so we react as if we're in danger. It's likely that when we're having a flashback our focus is fully on what we're internally experiencing and the vivid memory that we're going through, rather than on what's actually happening around us at that time. So, we could be in our safest place, with absolutely no threat near to us, but feel as if we're in a den of lions!

One of the best ways to help us feel safe again is to turn our attention away from our internal senses and towards our external senses (what's happening around us). This can mean doing grounding strategies (like the ones above). But it can also mean looking around us, noticing where we are and when it is (day, month, year, time), listening to what's happening and who is close by, and checking out whether the environment that we're actually in, right now, is safe.

This can be a bit of a step-by-step process:

Step 1: Acknowledge that you're having a flashback, which is a vivid memory (not the trauma repeating).

Step 2: Move your attention to external senses (notice when it is, and what's actually happening around you in the here and now).

Step 3: Based on what's happening 'right now', make a decision about whether you're safe, and if there's anything else that you need to do.

A flashback plan

It can be useful to make a bit of a flashback plan, which you can decide in advance and can be used when you feel a flashback coming on, or to reduce or end a flashback. You might find it useful to practise the plan on a regular basis, so that it feels more familiar to you (such as each morning when you get up). Or you might find it helpful to share it with someone close to you, so that they can talk you through it when you're having a flashback. Sometimes people also record a copy on their phone, so that they can play it back to themselves, without needing to think or remember, or read, at the time.

A flashback plan will be unique to you, depending on what works for you, but here is an example:

LUCY'S FLASHBACK PLAN

I'm having a flashback, which is a memory of the bad stuff that happened in the past. Years ago. I'm safe now and I've survived it.

I'm feeling...and I'm experiencing...because I'm remembering what happened when I was assaulted.

Right now, I can see...[five things], I can hear...[five things]...and I can physically feel...[five things].

Today is [day, date, month, year] and I'm safe now.

I will take a few deep breaths and feel my stomach rise and fall, then get an ice-cold drink and hold it to my face.

These techniques are very useful when you're in a safe environment or around safe people. But, importantly, if you're not safe (after you've noticed what's going on around you), it's important to seek safety.

Dream completion

Sometimes when we're struggling with trauma memories, this can also lead us to have nightmares or night terrors. These disturbing dreams are one of the ways that our brain is trying to process the traumatic experience. It might be that you just have an occasional bad dream, but it might also be that you have one most nights and they can be quite distressing. Nightmares can even lead to us worrying about going to sleep, for fear that we may relive the distressing dream again. What we also know is that not sleeping can make us feel even worse! (as described in Chapter 5).

Nightmares may happen more immediately after the traumatic event, but then might start to fade or become less frequent over time. Often, they might be based on an intense memory of what happened that is being replayed again and again. Or they might be similar to what happened but with a bit of a twist.

So, one of the ways in which we can try to stop the nightmares is to rewrite them or give them a new ending.

Rewriting your nightmares

Step 1: At a time when you're feeling okay, and safe, write down your nightmare. You might want to do this with someone else there so that they can ask you questions to help you remember it and write it down clearly. Even just the process of writing it down can start to make it feel a little less powerful.

Step 2: Think about the ending of the nightmare. If you were to rewrite it, what sort of ending would you want it to have? What would you ideally want to happen? What would be a safer, alternative ending? Write out the nightmare again but this time with the new, more enjoyable ending.

Step 3: Now it's time to rehearse and practise the new ending. You can either just close your eyes and imagine the new ending happening, or you might want to ask someone to read the new end of the dream out to you while you imagine it.

Step 4: Keep a copy of your written dream with the new ending next to your bed, then read and reread it before you go to sleep each night. If you wake up, try to read through the dream again then. The most important thing is to keep practising it, so that your brain remembers it when you're next asleep, and it starts to replace the original ending.

There are also other ways that you can remind yourself that you're safe at night, such as having a grounding card next to your bed, with a statement on it that reminds you about the here and now; for example, 'It's 2023, I'm safe, I'm in my bedroom.' Or you might want to keep a picture that reminds you of a soothing memory, or even use your grounding smell.

Training your hippo

In Chapter 2, we learned about how the brain processes trauma memories and why sometimes it gets quite stuck. It might continue to act as if the trauma is still happening or is about to happen again, which can lead to you feeling that you're always switched on and about to react. The brain might not remember that the trauma has ended, and that you've survived it and are safe again. The brain might think that the bad stuff is still happening, which can lead you to experience flashbacks and intrusive memories when you experience a reminder of the trauma or something that makes you feel under threat. It can feel as if the bad stuff is happening right now.

So, in this section, we will look at three steps to training your hippo (the hippocampus, or part of the brain that 'time-stamps' memories – see Chapter 2) to remind it that the bad thing happened in the past and you're safe now. This will update your mind so that it recognizes that the trauma ended and the event lies in the past.

Step 1: Creating a mantra

It can be useful to start by writing your own mantra or brief saying, to remind yourself, and your hippo, that you've survived and are safe now. For example, 'I've survived, and I'm safe now. It's 2023.'

Or, 'I'm okay. The bad stuff happened in the past. I'm safe now.' Choose whichever words work for you.

Step 2: Write, or draw, your story following the trauma

Think about all the things that have happened in your life since the trauma occurred, and how things have changed. You might want to write these down as an epilogue (brief notes or a full story – whatever suits you) or draw these out, or even collect evidence such as photos. Focus on things that will help your hippo to know that the trauma has ended, you survived it and life has continued since.

You might want to start writing about what happened just after the trauma and carry on in a chronological way up until now. Or you might want to start writing/drawing about now, and then go backwards. Whichever you prefer. Or you might want to just write or draw a list of what has changed.

It can be useful to think about what will let you know that things are different to what they were back then. You might, for example, notice how your hair is different now (longer or a different colour), that you're perhaps taller or your hands have grown bigger since it happened. Or even how your age has changed (e.g. I was 12 when it happened, but I'm 15 now).

Example epilogue: Since the 'bad stuff' happened

I was only ten when it happened and was still at primary school, but I'm at college now, so over six years have passed. I was so much smaller than I was now, and since then I've grown a lot stronger too and have started dancing and going running. Since then I've had about five proper holidays, a few in Wales and a couple abroad. I've also got a completely new group of friends, and none of them knew me back then.

Step 3: Acknowledge and celebrate that you survived

This might sound like a strange one, but one way to let your hippo know that the trauma happened a while back and you survived it is to give it a clear memory of your survival.

This could be a really good excuse to have a bit of a celebration or a party, or just a small meal with family and friends. Or it could be that you want to do some sort of ritual that has meaning to you, that recognizes that you survived. You might want to buy yourself a small gift, or someone else might buy something for you that you can keep (e.g. sometimes people might buy a bracelet that has a saying or symbol on it that reminds them of survival). Or you might want to make a piece of art of some sort, or write a song or piece of music, again to remind your hippo that you've survived. Your hippo can be very forgetful about this, so may need prompting a little!

You can do a celebration or acknowledgement at any point following the traumatic event, it doesn't have to be when everything feels okay again. It's just to celebrate your life and your ability to get through things, even if they still feel tough to cope with.

Chapter 10

Taming Your Blaming and Shaming

On top of all the trauma reactions that we've talked about so far, one of the most difficult ways that trauma can affect us is how it can make us feel bad about ourselves. Lots of people who have experienced trauma also feel shameful, and sometimes this feeling can stick around and make it hard for us to be able to move forward.

When we can start to forgive ourselves, and be compassionate towards ourselves, then this can help us to feel much better.

What do we mean by shame?

Often when we have experienced difficult things in our lives, we can start to believe that it must be our fault, or that we must have done something bad and therefore deserve what happened. You might have heard people saying, 'Why me?' When the answer to this isn't easy, or doesn't make sense, we then often assume that it must be something to do with us, that we must have done something wrong to cause the bad thing to happen. Or even worse, we might think that the bad thing happened because we're bad and we deserve it.

From a young age, we learn that we need to keep an eye on what we do and how we behave so that we don't upset or anger other people. So, when bad things happen later in our lives, and these things are hard to make sense of, we often naturally blame ourselves for them and feel shameful. We also worry about what other people think of us, or how they might react if they were to find out.

Feeling guilty means that we believe that we've done a 'bad thing' but that we're generally an okay person. But feeling shameful means that we believe that we did a 'bad thing', or something bad happened, because we are a 'bad person'. We fear that if people find out what we've done, they might see our 'inner badness', so we must do whatever we can to avoid people finding out! Shame is often linked to lots of other emotions too, like sadness, emptiness, helplessness, powerlessness, anxiety and anger. It can make us feel really worthless. And it can lead to us feeling very, very alone.

Shame makes us feel physically horrible too. When we feel shameful, we often feel sick, we might feel some chest tightness or feel weighted down, with butterflies in our stomach, or we might notice our face start to blush and feel hot and clammy. We often over-think things and have the urge to shrink or hide and look away from people. We know that our emotions are there to let us know when something is wrong, and they tell us when we need to react in a different way to protect ourselves. With shame, this then gives us the chance to avoid what's making us feel bad or do something differently next time.

Shame is often experienced by people who have been through trauma and bad experiences. We can often blame ourselves for what happened, or feel that we should have done things differently, or that we should be coping in a better way. We may feel that other people will judge us for what's happened. We may feel that we should have protected ourselves or fought back more or believe that we have let ourselves down during the trauma due to the way that we acted. All of this is completely normal and understandable, but also really difficult to get past.

We might also feel guilty because we worry that what we've experienced is 'not as bad' as other people have experienced, so we shouldn't be complaining or being 'overly dramatic'. Or we might feel that we should be coping better than we are doing, or even feel bad about the ways in which we're coping with the traumatic event, such as getting irritable with other people, or struggling to move on, or comfort eating, even though everyone copes differently with things and is affected by things in different ways.

Often experiencing trauma may also impact on the way that we see ourselves (see Chapter 3), and how we think that other people might view us. We might worry that we're 'damaged' by what we've experienced, or that other people will think that there's something wrong with us, that we're bad or even un-loveable, if they find out what has happened. This sometimes leads us to keep things to ourselves, and not talk about what's happened, due to a worry about people finding out and then rejecting us or seeing us in a negative way. When Reggie started at a new school, he didn't want to get too close to anyone at first, because he felt that he didn't deserve to be there and that he wasn't as good as anyone else. Feeling bad about ourselves can really get in the way of us building relationships and feeling close to other people.

How might shame affect our thinking?

When we feel shameful about things that have happened, this can affect the ways that we see ourselves and others and can lead to lots of different worries that can play on our mind. For example, we might be fearful that:

- people will find out what happened to us, and that if they do, they will think badly of us

- people might see us as damaged, bad or weak if they find out what happened

- we are damaged goods or contaminated in some way

- we are different, and are not good enough or are unloveable or deserve to be treated badly

- it's our fault that the bad things happened

- we caused them to happen because of the person that we are, or how we behaved

- we should have done something differently at the time that the bad thing happened

- we should be able to get on with things and move past the trauma, and that we're weak or useless for continuing to struggle.

Do you find yourself having any of the thoughts above, or anything similar? These are quite normal thoughts for people who have been through difficult times. We often tend to blame ourselves, rather than the person who hurt us. It can be useful to work out which thoughts are getting in the way of you being able to move on, then you can talk about them, challenge them and work through them.

How might shame affect what we do?

When we're feeling shameful, it can push us to act in three different main ways:

1. *Attack* – this can mean that we end up attacking (verbally or even physically) people before they have the chance to attack us. We can also try to keep people at a bit of a distance to keep ourselves safe. This means that we can end up being unfriendly or rude to other people so that they know to stay away from us. We might believe that people are going to end up judging or criticizing us, or seeing our inner badness, so it's safer to keep them away.

2. *Hide* – as we said above, often the urge that we get when we feel shame in our body is to shrink or hide. This can lead us to keep away from other people, avoid making friends or break friendships that we already have, making sure that we're always unavailable if people want to meet up. We

might think that if we keep away from people, we're less likely to be hurt.

3. *Trying to please* – we do whatever we can to try to please other people and do whatever they ask us to do. This way, we're trying to avoid upsetting or angering them at all. But this sometimes might lead us to do things that aren't fair or okay, that the other person has asked us to do. They might start to take advantage of us, but we put up with this, because we don't want to upset them.

All the above ways of coping make sense as they're our ways of protecting ourselves from bad things happening again. But often they can get in the way of us being able to live a fulfilling life in the future. Working on feeling safe in our relationships (when they're safe and trusting) is a really important skill, as feeling connected to others is a basic human need. See Chapter 4 about the importance of key relationships.

Why you were unable to stop the bad thing from happening

If you're feeling to blame for what happened to you, you're not alone. But also, forgiving yourself for what happened will be an important part of being able to move on. Often, if we look at the situation in a rational way, there's nothing really that you could have done to stop the bad things from happening.

There are lots of reasons why you might have been unable to stop the bad things from happening to you. It might be that you were in a powerless position, as you were younger, smaller or physically not strong enough to prevent it happening. It might be that you were outnumbered at the time, or that there was no one around you who could help, or someone coerced, threatened or even lied to you.

It might be that it was an accident, there was a mistake made or something bigger happened that was completely out of your control (e.g. a hurricane, a bomb), and you were unlucky enough to be there at the time that it happened. There might not have been any warning that it was going to happen, and it might have been a bit of a shock that you understandably didn't foresee.

We also know that often when people experience bad things happening, it can lead to them having trauma responses in the moment to help them to survive. But this means that you may have been frozen on the spot or zoned out, allowed things to happen (been 'compliant') to protect yourself from things getting worse, or tried to run away. Often people aren't able to fight back or shout out for help when the bad thing is happening. In fact, most people don't. When you experience some sort of threat, as we learned in Chapter 2, your threat system needs to make a decision really quickly about what to do in order to help you to survive. So it does this super quickly, without you even having time to think about what to do. Sometimes it doesn't make sense for you to use your 'fight' response, as it might not lead to a good outcome, for example if this would mean fighting against someone who is bigger or more powerful than you. But this sometimes means that you end up reacting by running away, zoning out or playing dead, which may have led you to be powerless to stop the bad thing from happening. These are absolutely normal and understandable responses when under threat. Luckily, we can update our survival response with new ways of reacting through physical training, which is discussed in Chapter 8.

Do any of these apply to you, and what you went through? If yes, make a note of them as they will be useful for the rest of this chapter.

How to work through feelings of shame

As we found out above, shame is an emotion that is linked to our beliefs about how other people see us. So, one of the best ways of being able to work through feelings of shame is to talk to someone about it.

The first step is to think about who you can talk to. It may be useful to talk to someone (ideally an adult, as they might have more life experience and have more idea of what to do) who you feel that you can trust and talk openly with, and who is caring and supportive towards you. This might be, for example, a family member or a tutor at school.

It can be really difficult to talk to people at first, especially if you're feeling shameful, as you might worry about how the other person will react. Reggie never used to talk to people when he was feeling rubbish, and would bottle it up, which made him feel worse. He didn't tell his parents, as he was worried about what they might think, and how they might react, and scared that they wouldn't want him anymore. But he's able to talk to his parents now, which helps a lot.

It can then be useful to ask them if you could have some space to talk with them about some things that you find difficult to talk about. Let them know what you want from the conversation (e.g. someone to listen and help you to make sense of things), so that they don't jump into 'problem-solving mode'. It can be helpful to have an activity to do when you're talking, such as going for a dog walk, cooking tea together or eating cake.

It can be useful to talk to them about the things that feel the least difficult first, then you can slowly work up to the more difficult stuff when you feel ready. But take things at your own pace.

It's okay to be angry

Lucy shares her personal experience:

> I always used to find it hard to blame anyone else for things that happened. If something went wrong, or I got hurt, I always felt that it was my fault, and that I must have caused it in some way. I never doubted this. My boyfriend usually told me it was my fault too, so I believed him. I felt so bad about myself and felt that I was to blame for staying in that relationship so long. It was toxic, and now I can see that. But even now, I can find it hard to shake the belief that when I was hurt it wasn't my fault. I think that things became a bit easier when I talked to my close friend about what had happened, and how I was still struggling with feelings of guilt and believing that I was to blame. She helped me to see that I was being controlled and made to feel that it was my fault when it was not. I was so glad that I talked to her. The next feelings that bubbled up for me were relief (that it wasn't all my fault) and pure anger that he had put me through this for so long. I tried to cope with this in many ways – by talking to friends, by going to the gym and burning off some energy, and by reading up on violence in relationships and finding out that there are a lot of other people out there who feel like me – that was reassuring. The other thing that helped was when a friend suggested that I write a letter to my ex, but without ever sending it, I could write down whatever I felt and thought about him (there was a lot!) without the fear of what might happen if he were to find out. It felt freeing. I then read it out to a friend, which was quite emotional, and then I tore it up. I realized that my feelings of, well, rage towards him were quite normal and understandable, and this helped me to start to let them go and move on with my life.

As Lucy describes, as you start to work through your feelings of self-blame or shame, you might notice some other emotions start to appear such as anger or upset towards others who were involved in the traumatic event. This again is completely normal and understandable. It can be useful to talk through these feelings with someone else, or as above, to write down your feelings in letters (without sending them). Another way that you could do this is to pick a chair that you want to represent the person who hurt you (an empty chair). Think about what you would want to say to that person, what you would want them to know, without them being able to talk back to you. You might want to jot down a few notes first, or even write a letter to read out. Then talk to the empty chair imagining that it's the person who has hurt you, which gives you the chance to let your emotions out and say the things that you might not have had chance to say. You might want someone else there at the time for support, or to plan a nice activity for afterwards. Talking to a chair might sound a bit strange but there's something quite different and powerful about hearing your words out loud rather than just thinking them.

Challenging your self-blame

We can often be much more compassionate and understanding to other people than we are to ourselves, so this last section focuses on thinking about how to be more wise, non-blaming, understanding and compassionate to ourselves too. You might want to go through this section with a trusted adult, who can help you to reflect on and answer some of the questions below to help you to get a more balanced (less self-blaming and more understanding) way of thinking.

It's best to have a go at this exercise when you're feeling quite calm and relaxed, and aren't likely to be distracted, so you can give it some real thought.

So, first of all, think about someone close to you, who you really care about. Imagine that they recently went through the bad thing that you've been through and are feeling shameful and to blame.

- How would you feel about them?

- Would you see them as responsible for what happened? If not, why not?

- If yes, how would you suggest that they could repair the situation and make things better?

- How would you react towards them when they told you? How would you speak to them? Would you try to comfort and support them, or would you be drawn to judging and blaming them?

- What would you say to that person? What would you want them to know?

- Is your response to your friend similar to how you've responded to your own feelings of guilt and shame? If not, consider why not. Why would things be different for you and them?

It can also be useful to think about what someone who you feel close to would say if they heard you talk about how you're feeling, and your feelings of shame and self-blame. How would they react? What would they be likely to say?

Another way to do this is to pretend that you're in a court trying to argue for and against your belief. It can be useful to do this exercise with someone close to you. So, initially, you might be the prosecutor trying to find the evidence to argue that your belief is true (e.g. that you're to blame and it's all your fault), while the person that you're doing the exercise with challenges this by asking you questions to make you try to defend this evidence. Does this evidence hold up against the questioning? Then swap, and this time be the defence. Think of all the evidence that the belief can't be true, and again the other person can help you to do this or ask challenging questions while you defend the evidence that the original belief isn't true. Then finish by together thinking about what an alternative, more realistic, belief could be.

There might be a few people reading this chapter who may have caused bad things to happen to other people, even if this was unintentional. If this is the case, it's likely that you will need to work through any feelings of regret and make attempts to repair your relationship with the other people involved. It may be difficult to forgive yourself until you've made efforts to try to make things okay again with the other person.

◇ Chapter 11 ◇

Avoiding Avoidance

We've already talked in Chapter 3 about why you might want to avoid even thinking about what's happened to you, never mind be around the places, people or things that you associate with a traumatic event. At the beginning, these reminders or 'triggers' can set off all sorts of reactions that we've talked about in this book so far – like overwhelming distress with horrible feelings in your body, flashbacks and/or dissociative experiences. It's a helpful response for you to take your time thinking about and being out in the world and around these triggers. This means that you have the chance to make sense of what's happened and to allow your brain and body the time they need to recover and heal without being overwhelmed. Slowly beginning to share with others some of your thoughts and feelings helps you to tell the story of what's happened to you and find ways to live with it.

Sometimes, the way that trauma impacts us means that we totally withdraw from the world for a while and then it can be scary and overwhelming to get back into the world and carry on living our lives. If you've recently experienced a traumatic event and are reading this book, then we would urge you to:

- get yourself into a routine as soon as possible

- with a trusted adult or friend, draw up a plan for each week, and, if you need to, break your days up into short time slots like 30 minutes or at most an hour

- not push yourself too hard, but to build it up and do small things. For example: 'My goal for 9–10am is to get out of bed and go downstairs. My goal for 10–11am is to have something to eat and brush my teeth.' A little is better than too much because then you're likely to give up if you feel overwhelmed. These small goals can help you to keep moving forward and not get stuck in one place and unable to move out of the 'flop' state

- remember the basics from Chapter 5 and try hard not to sleep during the day (keeping a sleep diary can be helpful to try and keep track) – some of your small goals can help with this too.

If it's been a while since you experienced your traumatic event/s and you're feeling stuck in flop (this might mean you're staying in your room, not leaving the house) and your world has become smaller, then all the things we've talked about so far are still helpful. If you've experienced a number of traumatic events or are now safe after living in a scary and traumatic house, community or even country, then it can take a little while before the reactions begin. They can even creep up on you and you suddenly find that you're not doing things that you used to do and are feeling trapped or stuck.

If this is the case, then use the ideas above and try to get back into a routine and make a realistic plan and goals for each hour (small things like brushing your teeth, getting something to eat, watching an episode of something that you like and makes you feel comforted). It can also be helpful to:

- make a list of things you used to like doing but have stopped doing. Think carefully about what would need to happen for you to start doing these things again. Pick the one you miss the most or are most motivated by and plan step by step what you need to do to get there over the next two weeks

- make a list of things you have maybe thought about trying or wanted to do but not had the time to have a go at

- put these things into your weekly planner – be kind to yourself and realistic. Start with five- or ten-minute activities. Don't start with big things that take lots of preparation or plan to do things for ages as you'll just make it more likely you won't manage it and that feels rubbish

- be consistent and remember that it's better to do something for a brief period of time than nothing at all

- train our minds to notice and value the small things and contributions. It's too easy to be a bit of a 'perfectionist' sometimes and not value the positives of small steps, activities and achievements

- connect with others and let them know how tough you're finding getting out of the house. Start just reconnecting through messaging them or ways that are less stressful and then begin to plan by making short phone calls to people you trust. If you feel confident, then make plans to spend time with people you feel safe with.

It is through getting out into the world and reconnecting that we can learn that we have agency (choices, control and influence) and can learn new skills, that we are connected to others and can have good friends and relationships, and that our emotions can be big and intense, but they don't last forever and we can actually manage them okay. These things are the key to resilience and they are much harder to find if you don't leave the house because you don't have any opportunity to discover 'Actually, I managed that'.

Breaking the cycle by facing our trauma triggers

This might be the part of the book where you are shouting in your head 'NO WAY! NOT A CHANCE! NOT HAPPENING!' Stick with us. We promise that you can do this if you just take it slowly and get the help of people around you. Research tells us that avoiding avoidance (exposure) is the key part in trauma recovery and reducing difficult feelings.

After a traumatic event, we can get stuck in threat brain, and if the threat is something we can't fight, then we're likely to try to get away from it or go into 'submit' or flop. It's one of the most efficient ways to avoid the horrible physical feelings that we are feeling after a traumatic event, and our evolutionary system is powerful.

Although we've talked about and recognize the value in taking things slowly and taking some time, why do we think you should start to do things that might set off some of your distress and difficult feelings? First, you need to have done all the things we talk about in Chapter 5 to be taking good care of yourself, and you also need to have some good coping and grounding strategies to be able to deal with some of your trauma reactions like flashbacks and dissociation. (If you haven't done these things yet we would urge you to go back and have a go before you start tackling some of your triggers head on.) But we are here telling you to do this, even though it's scary, because until you start to face the things that make your body and brain react with fear, you can't truly move on from the trauma. Here are seven reasons why facing your fears (now you've developed your coping strategies) is a way to heal and be able to get on with your life:

1. When you face your fears, you find out that you have the skills to manage the feelings and thoughts that come up, even if they are difficult and distressing. This feeling of overcoming can be empowering as well as hard. In fact, it being hard can make you feel more empowered!

2. If you can stick with the feelings of anxiety and distress, they will get less and you will realize that they don't last forever and are unpleasant but totally manageable – then the horrible feelings lose a little of their power too.

3. You only start to be able to accurately work out whether you're able to cope, and if bad things will really happen, when you get out there and try stuff out.

4. You are missing out – missing out on opportunities to connect with others and learn that although something terrible happened there are wonderful things in the world worth

taking risks for, and even when things are hard for a while, *you can cope.*

5. Every time you avoid the trigger you reinforce the idea that to be reminded of the trauma is unmanageable and will lead to bad things happening – so ultimately it makes it worse.

6. It's only through getting to a point where you can stay in a scary situation that you can just ride the wave of feelings and let them die out.

7. Being so scared of something because it reminds you of a trauma or difficult time so much that it interferes with your life is awful – but on the flip side, overcoming a fear is one of the best feelings ever! Your confidence will soar and this will likely have a positive impact on you in lots of ways.

Graded exposure – how does it work?

In days gone by, psychologists used something called 'flooding' to help people manage their fears. Avoiding things teaches us that we can't cope, that the feelings are unbearable and the trauma is still alive and can hurt us in some way. At some point in history, psychologists thought, 'Right, well we'll do the opposite, and instead of avoiding, we will drown in the feared thing.' If someone had experienced a terrible car accident, it was thought that sticking them in a car and driving till they stopped being scared would mean that their anxiety would peak and then begin to die out as they realized that this car wasn't going to crash like the other one did and they were going to be okay. For some people, this worked well, but for lots of people it didn't. Nothing works for everyone, but this was quite a high-risk strategy because if the person ended up feeling totally overwhelmed and getting out of the car, then their confidence was shattered and it gave weight to the idea that the trauma had made them unable to cope and that cars are too scary. When you're recovering from trauma you need to take care of yourself and face the things associated with your trauma slowly and with lots of support.

Graded exposure means slowly and in a thoughtful way facing up to the things that remind you of what happened and finding ways to cope with the traumatic responses (feelings in your body, dissociation, flashbacks). Facing your fears slowly in a planned way allows you to work with more manageable levels of distress and have time to manage and respond to your bodily reactions. It can also mean that you learn more about how you feel and react (the rise and fall of your emotions and sensations) and start to keep track of your thoughts while you are working towards overcoming a trauma trigger that you have been avoiding.

When we start young people out on an 'exposure ladder' we need a clear goal; for example, if you are avoiding being around people who remind you of the person who hurt you, it might be being able to go to a social event and talk to someone who has a beard like the person who hurt you. Work backwards from this goal to see what you can manage and how you can challenge yourself to get closer to the trigger and use all your healthy coping strategies (plus some treats and rewards) to allow yourself to face the trigger bit by bit. You might start with striking up a conversation with someone that you sort of know in a safe place and work up gradually through a range of situations until you are able to talk to a stranger who reminds you of the person who hurt you. Of course, this means you need to be getting out and socializing quite a bit, so you might need to do more work on the earlier part of this chapter first!

If you have avoided a trauma trigger for long enough, it can change so that you're not scared of something traumatic happening again, but more scared of what it does to your body and your level of anxiety. You become scared of the traumatic reaction, not the trauma. You can't control the world around you but you can take some control of what you do, think and feel when you are around things that remind you of the trauma – if you are willing to spend some time facing the fear and practising your coping skills when you are reminded of the trauma.

Designing your own exposure ladder

So, where do you start? You start with your end goal, and this needs to be something meaningful and important, because facing your fears can be tough and you need to feel motivated to do it. Make sure that your goal is clear and there is no confusion about what you want to be able to do. 'Feel myself again' doesn't really cut it and 'Not be scared of cars' is too vague. Think clearly identifiable behaviours and then think of a special treat or reward for yourself too – facing your fears is tough and you need to keep your motivation up. It can be useful to break the goal down into small steps, with each a small building block towards the end goal. If you can get a trusted adult on board this really helps with rewards, but make sure you reward yourself even if you are going solo. A nice meal out with family or a close friend or a trip to see a film or exhibition that you really fancy are great rewards, but you need to pick things that are going to be motivating for you.

Once you have a clear end goal, you need to work out the rungs on your ladder. Rate how scary each step is on a scale of 0–10 (0 being no fear at all and 10 the most terrified ever), to be sure that you are not trying to jump from things that are not really that scary and challenging, to things that are much tougher to face. It needs to build up gradually so that each time you are tolerating a little bit more distress and learning that it doesn't last forever, and you can cope with both the triggers and the feelings or reactions that it brings up. You can have between 8 and 12 steps on your ladder; usually it has about 10.

GRADED EXPOSURE FOR FEAR OF DRIVING THE CAR

END GOAL: To be able to drive for an hour to visit a friend.

Steps on my exposure ladder:

1. Watch YouTube videos where people are driving in the car together (3/10 fear)

2. Sit in the car alone not going anywhere (4/10 fear)

3. Sit in the car with someone in the driver's seat (5/10 fear)

4. Sit in the car with the engine running on the drive (5.5/10 fear)

5. Drive up and down a very quiet street for five minutes (7/10 fear)

6. Do the ten-minute drive to school/college (8/10 fear)

7. Drive to visit a relative 20 minutes away (9/10 fear)

8. Do the one-hour drive to friend's house (10/10 fear)

You need to decide exactly how long you are going to stick with the trigger or scary situation or what your 'anxiety rating' will be before you can quit. This often means staying in the situation for quite some time. We would usually say that you need to be rating your fear as less than 2/10 before you can call it quits. If you are feeling anxious enough for it to still make you feel nervous when you think about doing that step again, then you need to stick with it for a bit longer or just do the step again. For some steps, you may repeat them lots of times so that you can see and feel your level of anxiety and traumatic reactions come down below 2/10 before moving onto the next step, as you are not always able to control how long things happen for.

Managing setbacks

Sometimes when we talk to young people about exposure they say, 'I tried that and it hasn't worked.' More often than not, there is a really good reason that it hasn't worked and it isn't because they are immune to the power of facing their fears. Using exposure after you have experienced a trauma is not based on the idea that bad things will never happen again – sometimes they do, but what we learn through facing our fears is that the outcome we are scared of is not as likely to happen as we think it is, and that most of the time even when things go wrong, we can cope well enough to pick ourselves up and carry on.

Here are some common setbacks that get in the way of success-fully managing avoidance through an exposure ladder:

1. You don't really want to face the fear right now

It's not a good idea to start trying to tackle avoidance when you have a lot on. You need to have some time and not too many other pressures like exams or big changes in your life. If you're struggling to get going, maybe it's not the right time to start tackling your avoidance and you shouldn't give yourself a hard time, but just make a date (maybe after exams or during a holiday time) when you can reassess your situation.

2. The goals are not realistic

If you just have one thing that you are super scared of, then you probably just have to dive right in, but most people have a few. If you have started with something you are really terrified of, then maybe it would be good to start with a smaller fear. If the rungs on your ladder are well spaced then this shouldn't be too much of a problem, but if your anxious thoughts are screaming at you 'It can't be done!' when you think about your goal, then maybe you need a smaller, more achievable goal for your first go at exposure. Or maybe see obstacle 1 above – it might be that now is not the right time or your fear is serving another purpose.

3. The first rung on the ladder is too distressing and scary

A bit like obstacle 2, if you have something too scary on your first rung, it's hard to convince yourself to get started. You need something that is barely scary at all, then work your way up, with little rewards at every stop. If you're getting stuck, try to break steps down further.

4. The rungs between the ladder are too far apart

If you have big jumps between your steps, then you'll likely get stuck. If you're feeling 2/10 scared of sitting in the car on the drive with the engine running and 8/10 about actually setting off on the street, then there need to be lots of steps in between to build your confidence and help you learn that the trauma reactions and distress will go down and that you can cope with them. It can be that you're not used to rating anxiety on a 0–10 scale so aren't rating your feelings very accurately. It's fine to keep revising your ladder and adding steps or moving things around.

5. You are trying to move up the ladder too quickly

This is when you are eager to get over the trauma but forget that exposure is all about gradually allowing your distress to get better and learning that you can cope. If you manage a step then you can't just think 'Phew, I am so glad that is over' and move on to the next one; you need to feel that it is now a piece of cake and you could do it again in a flash. If you don't feel like this, then you haven't done that step for long enough or enough times.

Celebration time!

If you're thinking about and planning how to face your fears and avoid avoidance, then you need to really celebrate this and give yourself the credit that you deserve. This means you've worked through enough of your trauma reactions to be able to be brave and do the things that trigger them on purpose. You have the knowledge that you've developed enough skills and strategies to cope with the difficult thoughts and feelings that this might bring up, and can seek the help that you need to cope with what happens when you face your fears.

Facing your fears is a sign that you're really taking control and thriving after a traumatic event or the experience of separation and loss in your early life. Taking chances in your relationships and facing up to things like the possibility of rejection can be the hardest yet the most rewarding challenge, as you learn different ways to be with others where you feel more able to act in accordance with your values, not just your fear of rejection. When we make decisions about our relationships based on our fear of rejection, or act in ways that solely aim to avoid rejection, this can prevent us from getting close to others. But, when we can take a chance and not let our fear of rejection take over, this can help us to learn a different, more rewarding, way of being in relationships.

Chapter 12

What Next?

So, it might be that you've worked your way through this book, and you decide that you've done enough thinking about the past for now, that you're feeling pretty much okay, or that you're not ready to go into what happened in any more depth. It might be that by working through the book you've been able to get a bigger understanding of your own trauma responses and that these are normal, you know how to increase feelings of safety and stability to feel 'just right', and you are aware of ways to ground yourself in the moment, cope with difficult emotions and deal with any feelings of shame.

Some people won't need to do any specific trauma therapy, or may want to leave thinking about this until they're older and life is a bit more settled. Or it might be that you decide that you're ready to look into what else might help.

This chapter will aim to help you to think about whether you're ready for therapy; it will tell you about the different therapeutic approaches out there, so that you can think about what might be best for you, and what to expect if you do decide to go ahead. It will also have some young people's stories of going through trauma therapy.

Some of the main trauma therapies are eye movement desensitization and reprocessing (EMDR), trauma-focused cognitive behaviour therapy (CBT), dyadic developmental psychotherapy (DDP) and schema therapy, among many others. Psychologists love acronyms! We'll give a brief summary of these therapeutic approaches in this chapter.

Usually the goals of trauma-focused therapy are that:

- the trauma memories are no longer particularly distressing or fear inducing, or they don't bring on any difficulties like dissociation or flashbacks

- any things that have been triggering or would bring up intense memories and emotions associated with the trauma no longer do so

- you're able to live a 'normal' life and the past trauma is no longer affecting you day to day

- when you experience a stressful event, you can cope and recover from it without it bringing on a big stress response.

Are you ready for further therapy?

Most therapists will think with you about whether you're ready for therapy, and to talk about what happened, or if there's anything that needs to change to help you to feel safer first.

When you're starting to do some therapy around traumatic memories it can sometimes make you feel unsteady or wobbly. So, it's important that before you do this work, you have strategies (such as grounding strategies), you're generally looking after yourself (eating, sleeping, etc.) and you have people around you for support outside the sessions. This will help you to cope with the difficult emotions and memories that therapy sessions might bring up for you. It's also important for you to build a relationship with the therapist first before you get on to the trickier stuff.

Before starting therapy, you might want to consider these questions: Why are you thinking about doing this now? Is it because it feels like the right time to do it, or because you feel that you *should* do therapy? Is it because someone else has told you to go to therapy, or are you interested/curious about therapy even though you might feel a little unsure and nervous?

The main trauma therapies

Eye movement desensitization and reprocessing (EMDR)

EMDR is one of the most common therapies for trauma and there has been lots of research which has suggested that it can help young people who have been through traumatic experiences. It's also useful for low mood, anxiety and other problems too. This therapy takes into account how the mind is often able to heal itself in a natural way, especially when we're asleep. The type of sleep that tends to support healing the most is rapid eye movement (REM) sleep. EMDR notes that when you experience a traumatic event, difficult memories, thoughts and images can stay unprocessed and get stuck in your brain, causing difficult feelings and experiences. As we discussed in Chapter 2, these memories are often highly emotional, vivid and sensory, rather than verbal, and they don't have a 'time-stamp'. EMDR aims to create connections between the different parts of the brain that process memories, to help the trauma memories to be processed so that they can be 'filed away'. We still have the memories, but they aren't so 'active' and causing so much distress anymore.

EMDR can be done as a short-term therapy (e.g. six sessions) or can be part of a longer-term therapy intervention (e.g. 24 sessions or more). This will depend on the type of trauma/difficulties that you've experienced and how it's affected you. When you first meet with the therapist to talk about the therapy, they should be able to give you an idea of how many sessions might be useful for you. Each session would typically last for 60–90 minutes.

At the start of EMDR sessions, the therapist talks to you about trauma and how it affects the brain, body and memory processing (as we discussed in Chapter 2). Then they think with you about grounding strategies (see Chapter 9), building your resources and safe place imagery (similar to how this is described in Chapters 5 and 6). Then you go on to trauma processing. Any good EMDR therapist spends the first few sessions just thinking about building a safe place, grounding techniques and the resources that you have, and gives you time to build safety in your relationship with them.

You start by thinking of a memory that causes you some distress, for example 5/10. During an EMDR session, you are asked to hold in mind the worst bit of the memory, the image and what's going on in the image, any negative thoughts that you might have about yourself that fit with the image, and the emotions and sensations that you feel. You are then asked to rate the distress that you feel while thinking about the image, and then the therapist helps you to process the memory for a short time, while they regularly check in with you and asking, 'What do you notice?' To help you to process this memory, the therapist supports you to move your eyes in a similar way to how they would move when you're in REM sleep. This eye movement is called bi-lateral stimulation. For example, they might move their finger from side to side and ask you to follow it, or they might use firm tapping of your shoulders or hands. Often you can do this regular, rhythmic tapping yourself while the therapist guides you. Alternatively, they might ask you to follow moving lights with your eyes or use headphones or another visual cue. During this, you stay completely wide awake and alert, so you can stop it at any time if you feel uncomfortable. Once you have 'processed' the distress of the memory and no longer feel distress, you should feel more able to hold in mind a slightly more distressing memory, e.g. 7/10, building your confidence in a gradual way.

Afterwards, you might find that your memories start to become less painful or emotional, and that any trauma reactions (e.g. flashbacks or dissociation) lessen or stop. You might even find that several memories heal all at once, as they might be linked together in your mind, and so processing one of these memories helps lessen the impact of others associated with it (how clever is your brain?!). Once the memory is no longer distressing to you, the therapist works with you to strengthen more positive thoughts, feelings and sensations that you choose to associate with this memory instead; for example, 'I'm a good person' instead of 'I'm bad'.

It's important to know that although EMDR can be a really useful therapy, it can also bring up really difficult and intense feelings and thoughts during and after sessions. So, it's important to think about whether you feel ready to do this, and to ensure that you have support in place. Research shows us that exposure is the best way to reduce the impact of trauma and strong emotions, so it can be a really important part of therapy. What's useful about EMDR is that you don't have to talk a lot about the trauma compared to a lot of talking therapies.

CJ'S EXPERIENCE OF EMDR

You can take it slow and take care of yourself in the EMDR therapy process. You may want to rush in and get it done, but taking care of yourself and taking your time is important. This allows you to build a relationship with your EMDR therapist and really understand what you're feeling, allowing you and your EMDR therapist to understand what you need to work with. It's intensive and brings up a lot of thoughts and feelings for a few days surrounding the memory you've been processing in the session. This was difficult at first and it's important to make sure you do take care of yourself. Taking yourself away from stressful situations and into more enjoyable environments helps to manage this. Your EMDR therapist will stop every so often and ask what you notice (thoughts, feelings or sensations). Whatever comes to your mind during the processing of the memory is okay. Nothing is 'stupid' or 'wrong' and doing this does work. Afterwards you may feel tired and drained; but the feelings associated with the memory may have changed, which is really helpful. It changes the way you feel about the memory and 'turns it down'.

Trauma-focused CBT

Trauma-focused cognitive behaviour therapy (TF-CBT) is a therapy for young people which focuses specifically on trauma. It can be undertaken in 8–25 sessions, depending on the type of trauma, how it's affected you, and what resources you have in place. The sessions are usually split, so that some are completed with you and the therapist, and some are completed with your parent/carer and therapist (about half and half).

The therapy aims to help you to change any thoughts, feelings and behaviours that are unhelpful to you, and may be linked to the traumatic experience. Like lots of other trauma therapies, it starts with information about why we experience trauma reactions. Then parents have some sessions focused on parenting skills, communication and managing stress. You and your parent access some sessions around coping strategies; both emotional and cognitive coping. These include grounding strategies (see Chapter 9), and other coping strategies that can help you to get through the overwhelming feelings that trauma can bring, such as relaxation exercises. There's also some work with beliefs that you might hold about what happened and what this means about yourself, other people and the world. Sometimes going through trauma makes us see the world in a negative or biased way, so TF-CBT helps to challenge the way that we're thinking about situations, ourselves and others, and to see them in a more balanced way.

In TF-CBT, the therapist helps you to talk through, imagine, write or draw about what happened to you. For example, you might create a story with the therapist based on your experience, and this story is developed and enhanced until you find it much easier to talk through. Later in sessions, you share the story with your parent or carer, with the support of the therapist, to help them understand your perspective on what happened.

Schema therapy

Schema therapy can help us deal with trauma by better understanding the ways that we have come to protect ourselves from the experiences that we might have had in early life through the therapist doing something called 'limited re-parenting'. This doesn't mean the therapist tries to be your parent, it means they offer the 'good enough' relationship and support that you might not have had to help you deal with your difficult experiences when or after they were happening. This kind of therapy is most often used for young people who have experienced developmental trauma as they have often not had the relationships they needed to process their multiple traumas and fear of letting others in or fears of letting others go in case they don't come back. These patterns of relating need a longer-term therapy to help you develop enough trust in the therapist and their support of you to try out some different ways of understanding yourself and how you have learned to cope with your traumas and relationships. Schema therapy can use visualizations to help you access feelings and experiences from the past and also to get more understanding and feeling about things that might have happened between sessions. Schema therapy also uses 'chair work', where an empty chair enables you to think about different ways that you cope, or about yourself at different ages. This might all sound a bit weird but lots of adults who have experienced multiple childhood traumas find it very useful and there is hopeful research for young people being published all the time. Finding a schema therapist who works with young people can be a bit more difficult, but this could be worth looking at if you have experienced a lot of loss and trauma early in your life.

Dyadic developmental psychotherapy (DDP)

DDP is a type of therapy that involves two people (or sometimes three) and a therapist. Dyadic actually means the relationship between two people, because DDP is a therapy that helps with relationships. There's usually a child or young person with a key adult (a parent or carer).

In Chapter 1, we talked about the different types of trauma, and DDP is typically a therapy that is designed to help people who have experienced developmental trauma. The 'developmental' bit is because young people who have DDP often have not been well cared for by their family growing up, and sometimes may now live with new parents or carers. The reason why the parent or carer would attend with you is to help them to be able to better understand your experiences and how they can support you and help you to build a trusting closer relationship with them.

Often DDP is used with a young person who has been through trauma or difficult life experiences when they were a child, which may be difficult to understand or make sense of, and which might be affecting them still today. It recognizes that sometimes these traumatic experiences can affect relationships, including those with parents or carers, and it can make it hard to trust parents and allow them in (as we spoke about in Chapter 4). The therapy recognizes that sometimes it can be really difficult to talk about things that have happened in the past, and the therapist may help you by wondering aloud, making guesses and trying to make sense of things with you, checking things out with you along the way. It can help you to communicate things to your parent or carer which might be difficult to say.

Usually, the therapist meets with you and your parents/carers together, but there are likely to also be times when they might meet with you or your parents/carers individually to find out how things are going and how you're experiencing the therapy sessions.

Typically, a session involves talking about things that have been happening over the past couple of weeks, both good things and things that might have been more difficult, to find out more about you and your life. They might also reflect with you about how things that happen in your life now might also be linked to things that have happened in the past, and to try to create together a story that makes sense. Sometimes in DDP you also write a therapeutic story with the therapist, or they write a story to share with you.

JAMES'S EXPERIENCE OF DDP

I started therapy sessions when I was aged seven and have had sessions on and off since then. All that therapy has been with Kim (therapist). I stuck with her because she knew me, my family, my history, and she was willing to keep me on when I needed to go back. She knows me, or more or less everything about me, how I react to things, how I think, how I see the world, and what I've already dealt with. The most important thing to me has been the relationship with Kim.

When I started therapy, I'd stopped letting myself be looked after, and I was very independent, looking after my sister myself, as no one else was going to do it. In therapy, I unpacked the crap that was my childhood. DDP was hard. It was like having someone be like a terrier, making me sit with emotions that I wanted to ignore. I'm not going to sugar-coat it. But it was good too. You don't realize how it's helping at the time. I realize it a lot more now because I have much more understanding of life. You make sense of where you have come from, why you are talking and reacting to people in the way that you are; you work out your priorities. All those things that you are not thinking about, they all change and you feel a lot happier in yourself.

The therapist tells you stuff that you already know. It's hard to put into words, but she is a bit of a mirror. So she will ask you a question like, 'That's really hard. How does that make you feel?' Then it makes you be really reflective. It makes me think, why is that doing that? And then she says, 'Well it could be because...how does that sit?' And you're like, can you shut up now? Because that's exactly like it is! It was going at my pace, slow, challenging my own preconceptions. If there was something that I wasn't ready to talk about yet, she would acknowledge it, and then come back to it when I was ready. It wouldn't always be formal too. Sometimes she would bring her dogs and we would go for a walk around the village. She would ask how things were going with school and with my carers. It wasn't just about the past, it was based on me and where I wanted to go. No session was the same.

DDP is not like CBT where you're having to do some specific work and doing homework tasks. Instead, you stay in the moment and you go through what you talk through in the session, you make sure that you are okay at the end of it, you go off and live your life and see where you are at the next session. It is a slow, gradual mending or healing. It helps just being able to talk. If you want to chat and to challenge yourself, go down this route. But don't pigeonhole yourself. If it doesn't work for you, talk to your therapist and find something else that fits.

I have had DDP in my life for years, and I'm a big advocate for it. If you are thinking about doing DDP, be prepared to look at yourself fully. Remember that it's actually okay not to be okay; although this might sound a bit cheesy, it's true. If you're not happy with some stuff that you are seeing in yourself, that's not a problem. Accept that this is part of the journey, and it is a journey, not a quick fix. But if you want lasting results, this can work.

Reflections from Kim

When I first met James, he was trying so hard to take care of himself and his sister. It was really hard for him to trust any adult to help him. In some ways, he was easy to work with – he sat still and talked to me! In other ways, he was very hard to work with – he did not trust that therapy would be safe, especially if we talked about feelings! That is where I had to start, building trust. DDP is a therapy that focuses on the relationship the therapist has with the child, and taking the time needed to build this and to help the young person trust you and trust that therapy can be helpful. If we give this the time that it needs then we can work together on the tricky stuff. That is what James and I did. We got to know each other, we made sense of things together, we figured out all the defences that James had in place to keep himself safe, and also how those defences were not always helpful. Then James took the brave step of allowing those defences to drop when with me and his foster carer, and we could begin to work with his feelings. That was hard work but we did it together. James discovered that it was safe to feel emotion and to let people help you with this. That made him a stronger person. He started to feel more secure with safe adults, like me and his foster carer and some of his teachers. He didn't have to do it alone anymore. He then had me and his foster carer to help him make sense of what had happened in the past that made him want to hide his feelings away. By understanding his past, he freed himself from it and could become the person he was born to be.

If you are interested in DDP and are wondering if it is the right thing for you, have a look at a book my friend Hannah has written called *Deep Sea Diving: Exploring the Process of Therapy within the DDP Model*. You can request an electronic copy at this link: https://ddpnetwork.org/library/deep-sea-diving.

But what if you start therapy
and it feels too much?

It's really important that if you decide to go ahead with trauma therapy, you know that it's okay to stop or let the therapist/psychologist know if it's too much for you right now, or that you want to slow things down. That's absolutely okay to do.

Bridie and Sue, as psychologists, would truly prefer someone to let them know if the therapy feels too difficult or is not suiting them. Our message to anyone accessing therapy would be that the therapy is for you, not the therapist. So, it's important that you're finding it helpful. Although it might sometimes feel difficult to do, it's fine to let your therapist know that it's not working for you.

It might be that you just want to stop for now, but that an extra session or two could be used to help you to feel safe and okay again; that it's just not the right time for you, and you're feeling too overwhelmed by it all; that it's all a bit too fast and intense and you want to slow down a bit; that you and the therapist aren't a good fit, or you don't feel that you have a good enough relationship with the therapist to trust them or feel safe. It could be that this just was not the right therapy for you, so you could think about what other potential options might be. If you want to let your therapist know that you want to stop sessions, or that the therapy doesn't feel right for you, there are different ways to do this. You could tell them when you see them if that feels okay to do, or you could send them an email or message.

Chapter 13

Surviving to Thriving: Post-Traumatic Growth

> *Look what was sown by the stars*
>
> *At night across the fields*
>
> *We are not defined by scars*
>
> *But by the incredible ability to heal*
>
> (Taken from *My Name is Why: A Memoir* (2019) by Lemn Sissay – printed with permission from the author.)

Most of the book so far has focused on how difficult and upsetting the impact of post-traumatic reactions can be. It's also important to think and talk about how the process of healing after trauma can lead to lots of positive changes too. Psychologists and others working with trauma call this 'post-traumatic growth'. The research about growth and healing after trauma tells us that even if you're suffering with lots of the difficult effects of trauma we have talked about in this book, you can still experience the positive impact too. In fact, it's thought that the growth comes out of the tough bit where you struggle with what has happened and how it has affected you, and where you make sense of what has happened and how best to move your life forward.

Kintsugi, or kintsukuroi, is a Japanese art where broken pottery is put back together. However, rather than hiding the cracks, these are decorated so they are more obvious and seen as beautiful, telling a story, and having a unique history. The cracks are painted gold, silver or platinum to create 'golden joinery'. This process is important when thinking about how trauma affects us. There's sometimes an idea that 'recovery' means that we're trying to get back to how things were before the trauma, that we need to 'get back' to being the person we were. But that is not the case. As humans, we're always changing and adapting to fit with the world around us and to what is happening to us. When we start to move on from a traumatic event, we're in fact a new, changed, but often wiser and stronger, version of ourselves who might have a better understanding of who we are/want to be and what is important to us. It can be helpful to not talk or think about 'getting back' to how we were before, but instead think about how we can use what we have learned about ourselves and the new ways of coping with difficult thoughts, feelings and things that happen to make our lives going forward healthier and more fulfilling.

This chapter will now give you some information about common types of 'post-traumatic growth' that people who have experienced trauma have talked about.

Personal transformation

After experiencing a traumatic event, our minds and bodies start to try to adjust to the new circumstances that we're living in. Our beliefs, emotions and relationships, and understanding of our lives, flex and change to take into account what we've been through and how we've made sense of it.

Generally, as humans, as we age, we tend to start to become wiser as we learn more about ourselves, other people and the world. But, when we've been through trauma, this can often really speed up this learning and gaining of wisdom (you don't have to be old to be wise). It literally can be life changing, but in a good way. The things we learn about ourselves, other people and the world can help us to find new purpose and meaning in our lives, it can help us to know how we can cope with things better and solve problems that we may come across. It can also help us to learn more about who we are and strengthens our sense of self and the meaning in our life story. Trauma can also impact on our beliefs about what life is all about, which can lead to spiritual change and a change in religious beliefs too. In young people, it's been suggested that post-traumatic growth can also lead to a development in qualities that are going to be real strengths such as perseverance, honesty, bravery, curiosity, learning, creativity, beauty and zest.

I'm a survivor! (Resilience and personal strength)

Resilience is all about 'bounce-back-ability'. This means, being able to bounce back and cope when going through difficult events. It doesn't mean that things will not affect you – they will – but that you feel stronger and able to return to what matters and what you value more quickly because you are more able to cope with what life throws at you.

When we've gone through a traumatic experience, this can lead to us finding and building our inner resilience and personal strengths. This then means that we'll be more able to cope with any future trauma or difficult experiences, because we're better prepared and know how best to cope with them. When we've been through something so difficult, it can make us realize how amazingly strong we actually are, and all that we can actually get through, increasing our self-belief about getting through things in the future.

Lauren shares her personal experience:

When the pandemic happened, it was like my worst nightmare. I have always worried in my younger life SO MUCH about getting sick and germs. But having been really ill, going through a painful and traumatic treatment, but surviving all of that, it was surprising how easy it was for me to cope with. I think because I had already survived something that truly felt like the end of the world, I felt like

I had some armour. I mean, I not only survived it but managed to find peace through podcasts and mindfulness apps when I would never have believed I could have! Mostly, I found strength and happiness through connecting with people who make me laugh but also don't mind when I cry. I cannot believe how well I have coped with the last 18 months. I guess I really did learn a lot through being so scared.

German philosopher Nietzsche once said, 'What doesn't kill me, makes me stronger', which means that when we've been through difficult life events, this can increase our feelings of strength. One important change when we're moving through trauma reactions is the change from a belief about being a 'victim' (someone to whom something bad was done) to being a 'survivor' (someone who was able to get through some really difficult things). This change in perception in seeing ourselves as surviving or overcoming can improve our self-esteem and self-belief, and make us see ourselves as powerful and full of courage and strength.

Sometimes people think that bad things will never happen to them, so they may think 'why me?' or feel shocked and paralysed when something difficult happens. This can then really shake up their sense of self and others, and the world. The most resilient people know that bad things happen sometimes, and that although they can be really difficult and will affect us, we can get through (survive) them. We can get through anything! This realization that difficult things can and do happen, and we're likely to experience difficult things in our lives, helps us to be able to face things in the future.

Making the most of our lives

Going through trauma can also lead us to feel more grateful for our day-to-day lives, and even for life in general. Sometimes it can bring everyday things into more focus for us, and we may start to be more able to find smaller things to appreciate in our everyday experiences. When we know how fragile life can be, it can lead us to realize that it's worth living and appreciating as much as we can. So, we can start to value our lives, and the people around us, more. We may even start to feel privileged to be able to live each day.

As going through difficult things can shake up our sense of ourselves and the world, it can also sometimes lead us to start to question our day-to-day lives. We may see the fragility of life and want to start to think about how we can live life to the full. Or we may want to think about what we want to work towards, focus on and achieve. It may also lead us to focus more on our values (what's most important to us) which can shift our everyday focus more on to things that are more meaningful to us, such as family, friends, helping others or achieving something in particular.

Sometimes the personal strength that we talked about above may also give us a sense that if we can get through what we've done, we can achieve anything! This can lead to a 'can do' attitude where we may feel more confident to go for what we want.

More meaningful relationships

Although earlier chapters talk about how trauma can potentially negatively affect our relationships, over time we may find that our relationships have strengthened and become even more important to us. Particularly for young people, going through traumatic events can lead us to feel closer in our relationships with people that we trust. Trauma can change our priorities about who, and what, is most important to us in life. It's likely that other people who are close to us, and whom we trust, have been essential in helping us to get through the traumatic memories. Over time, we may start to realize who is most important to us, to choose more carefully who we spend time with and build closer and more meaningful relationships with those that we care about and trust. Our close friends, family and others may become our greatest support, but also, we may start to appreciate them even more, and be grateful for their connection with us. We may have deeper, more meaningful conversations with them, as we start to create a new narrative for ourselves about life in general. We may also become more discerning with relationships that just don't feel right.

Increased skills/toolkit for coping

When we've been through traumatic experiences, we may end up with an increased variety of coping skills and strategies and start to know which ones work best for us. So, the next time that we face something difficult, we may feel more prepared and confident that we've got skills that work for us. We may also feel more confident in making decisions or seeking support from those around us when we need it (because we've had to do it before so have learned how to).

Self-reflection, empathy and compassion

Through the process of making sense of what happened, we're likely to have gained some personal insight and a greater self-awareness. This ability to reflect and understand ourselves and others better is a higher-level thinking skill which fits with emotional maturity and resilience. This can lead to feelings of compassion towards ourselves, and also to other people. We may feel a deep empathy for other people going through difficult times and better understand what they may feel. Lots of people in caring professions, such as psychologists, have been through their own trauma, found a way to heal and wish to use this experience to support other people.

How does post-traumatic growth happen?

One of the biggest learnings about post-traumatic growth is that it's a process. It's not something that is either there or not, but something that can start to develop over time, as we start to make sense of what we have been through, and this impacts on our understanding of ourselves, the world and others.

The process can change feelings of disappointment into gratitude and a greater appreciation of the world. It can change a belief of being a 'victim' into being a 'survivor'. It can move feelings of having no control into feelings of strength ('I can get through this!'), and feelings of being fragile to feelings of being powerful and courageous.

Perhaps weirdly, we can learn to feel both more vulnerable than we were before while also feeling more powerful – 'Bad things happen that will affect me AND I'm strong and can get through them.'

Research reveals that following traumatic experiences, we tend to go through a great deal of emotional stress and our sense of ourselves, other people and the world is often shaken (see formulation information in Chapter 3). To get to post-traumatic growth, we go through a process where we start to make meaning of what's happened, creating wisdom and changing our life story. At first following an event, there's a period of rumination (thinking intensely about what happened). Often this will include thinking about why the trauma happened, lots of 'what-if' thinking (see Chapter 3), and wondering whether there's any way that the traumatic event could have been avoided or escaped. This intense thinking can be a way of trying to feel more in control following the difficult event. If we're someone who feels they need to try to take control a lot to feel safe, this is a stage we can get a little stuck in sometimes. Knowing this about ourselves can help us to notice this stage and let it go.

Then we start to express our feelings or share them with others. This might be through being creative, writing things down or doing art, or through talking to other people close to us. We sometimes feel compelled to do this, as it's an important part of starting to make sense of what has happened. Sometimes we will also write things or get involved in a cause that has something to do with what we have been through. This 'doing something' can help us to feel more in control of our emotional distress, and by writing, creating or talking things through, we are starting to self-analyse, which can help us to develop a greater understanding and awareness of ourselves, and what happened.

The expression of emotions can often help us to transform too. Research shows that where people initially feel guilt or shame (see Chapter 10), this can move into feelings of anger, and then finally feelings of acceptance. But it's important to note that everyone is different and will go through different, and often a range of, emotions as they come to terms with what they have been through.

How can you help it along a bit?

There are a few different ways that the research suggests can help you to experience post-traumatic growth:

- Do something artistic or creative. This could mean drawing or creating something which helps you to express your emotions, or creating music. When we do creative things that help us to manage our emotions and be creative, this may support with the growth. Also, it's been argued that going through trauma can also increase our creativity too!

- Write things down, whether this is writing in a diary/journal, doing a formulation (as in Chapter 3), or just writing down whatever comes into your head. You might want to keep this private, or to share it with people close to you, so that they can help you to make sense of your thoughts.

- Talk to other people that you trust about your thoughts and feelings about what has happened. It's been suggested that when we talk to others, they can help us to explore different perspectives on what has happened, and they can show us empathy, compassion and acceptance. They can enable us to process difficult emotions that we may be experiencing, such as shame or upset, and can help us to know that other people may go through similar things too. When people have been through similar experiences themselves, this can also give us a sense of being understood and belonging, or we may see them as good role models.

- Have a go at your formulation (see Chapter 3) as a way of starting to make sense of what happened to you and how you got through it.

- Access therapy to make sense of what you have been through, and how your traumatic experiences may have impacted on your sense of self, other people and the world (see Chapter 12 for more information about different thera-peutic approaches). One of the processes of post-traumatic growth is called 'self-analysis' through rumination, which is about thinking about how the trauma may have affected you (including your thoughts and feelings), and making sense of what has happened, giving the experience new meaning, and integrating it into your general understanding of yourself, life and the world. This can then lead to a kind of resolution, which supports personal transformation.

- When the anger stage comes, express this physically (safely), perhaps using a punch bag, punching a pillow, running or pressing your palms together.

- Use your knowledge about what happened to help others, or to try to prevent something similar happening in the future. This could include, for example, getting involved in a campaign about road safety, fundraising for a domestic violence charity, or creating some resources about bullying.

Survival, growth and beauty

So, at the end of this book, we want to highlight that although going through traumatic experiences can be incredibly distressing and leave some ongoing reactions, there's also the potential for significant growth. Like a kintsugi pot, when put back together with some care and sparkle, we can grow stronger, and more self-aware, compassionate and beautiful.

Appendix I: Criteria for Post-Traumatic Stress Disorder (PTSD)

Criterion A: Exposure to stressor (recognition of direct or indirect exposure)

- Direct exposure to the traumatic event

- You witnessed the traumatic event

- You learned of a traumatic event

- Repeated or extreme indirect exposure to a traumatic event

Criterion B: Intrusion symptoms (experience of at least one of the following)

- Recurrent memories of the traumatic incident

- Traumatic dreams in relation to the traumatic event

- Dissociation symptoms which include flashbacks (feeling as if the traumatic event is happening again in the present moment)

- Psychological distress caused by cues that serve as reminders of the traumatic event

- Strong physiological reaction to reminders of the traumatic event

Criterion C: Persistent avoidance (at least one of these two criteria)

- Avoiding thoughts, feelings and physical sensations which trigger memories of the traumatic event

- Avoiding external reminders of the traumatic event which can include people, places and activities

Criterion D: Negative alterations in cognitions and moods (at least two of the following)

- Dissociative amnesia – not being able to remember important aspects of the traumatic event

- Persistent and negative beliefs or cognitions about self, other people or the world – I'm a bad person, or the world is an unsafe place

- Persistent cognitive distortions in relation to blaming self or others for causing or consequences of the traumatic incident

- Negative trauma-related emotions – for example, shame, anger, guilt or fear

- Loss of interest in activities or interests once enjoyed

- Feelings of detachment or estrangement from others

- The inability to experience positive emotions – for example, happiness and love

Criterion E: Alterations in arousal and reactivity (at least two of the following changes)

- Irritable or aggressive behaviour

- Self-destructive, impulsive or reckless behaviour

- Feeling in a hypervigilant state – feeling as if constantly on guard

- Exaggerated startle response – being startled easily

- Problems concentrating

- Problems sleeping

Criterion F: Duration of symptoms

- 'Acute distress disorder' symptoms are experienced for longer than one month

Criterion G: Functional significance

- The symptoms impair social function, occupation and other areas in everyday living

Criterion H: Exclusion

- The symptoms aren't attributable to medication, substance use or illness

★

___

Appendix II: A Template for Writing Your Own Formulation

> You can download this template from www.jkp.com/ catalogue/book/9781839971280

My story (see Chapter 3 for prompts)

What's happened to me? (What are my life experiences?)

....

....

....

....

....

What am I really scared of? (What pain/fear might I be trying to avoid or protect myself from?)

....

....

....

....

....

What am I doing to cope in the best way I know how? (What am
I doing to cope with the fears above? How am I protecting myself
against them?)

....

....

....

....

....

What are the unintended consequences of my ways of coping?

....

....

....

....

....

What are my protective factors? (What helps me to cope in a positive way/feel better?)

....

....

....

....

★
———

Appendix III: Information for People Close to You

You can download this template from www.jkp.com/catalogue/book/9781839971280

Here are some top tips from young people who have been through difficult experiences that they wished the adults (including professionals) had known when they were supporting them through trauma.

I wish that the adults had known that...

- even as a teenager with lots of friends it can be hard to talk to them about traumatic experiences, so adults might be the only people who I can share my thoughts and feelings with

- just because you are a grown-up doesn't mean you have to fix things or have the answer. The people who help the most are just easy to talk to – people who are easy to talk to don't butt in or interrupt, they just sit and listen and say 'I want to help' or 'I am so glad you told me' but don't pretend they have all the answers or can make it all better

- to be able to talk to you I need to know for sure that you are interested and care about my feelings – even the difficult ones. I know this when you are available to me and ask about me and what is going on in my life

- often I am struggling to understand what is happening, so please don't ask 'Why?' when I do or say things. It can feel as if you are judging me

- when people say 'You should talk to X about this' (e.g. your therapist or a certain teacher) it can feel as if you don't want to talk to me

- where we talk always needs to feel safe and be private and away from others – the place is nearly as important as the person (but not as important)

- too many questions can feel too much and make me shut down

- sometimes talking doesn't help and I need support in another way, like eating together or watching a movie together. Doing things and playing games can help me calm down just as much as talking

- trying to make things better can often make things feel worse. We just want to be listened to and to know that you are there. We don't want to be told that things are going to be okay because that can feel impossible to believe when something really bad has happened

- when you don't always have time for me it can then feel hard to talk at the 'right' time when you are free

- I don't want lots of small talk that can feel dismissive, but I also need you to be careful about talking directly about the past because that can be too much and cause me to have trauma reactions like flashbacks and become disconnected or even dissociated

- you really need to know and understand me before you start making links between what is going on now and what happened in the past because I feel upset and not understood when adults get this wrong.

Appendix IV: UK Helplines/ Websites for Support

If you're in immediate danger, call your emergency services and ask for the police.

In the UK, this means dialling 999. If you're not safe to speak, you can stay on the line and then press '55' when prompted to be put through to a 'silent solution' service. The call handler will then ask you some questions and let you know how to respond (saying yes or no if you can, or pressing certain keys).

If you're in an abusive relationship and need immediate help, you can also go into a pharmacy which has an 'Ask for ANI' logo on display somewhere. You can ask staff for ANI, and they will know that although it sounds as if you're asking for Annie, you're actually asking for 'Action Needed Immediately'. They will then offer you a private space to talk, give you a phone to use, and ask if you need support from other services (such as the police or support services).

Here are some of the helplines/agencies that people in the UK have reported finding most useful:

Childline: by phoning 0800 1111, you'll get through to a counsellor; they're there to listen and support you with anything you'd like to talk about, or you can have an online chat with a counsellor.

Crimestoppers – an independent charity that gives people the power to speak up about crime, completely anonymously: 0800 555 111.

Frank: phone the 0300 123 6600 helpline, text 82111 or email frank@talktofrank.com to have a confidential conversation about drug and alcohol use. There is also a webpage with lots of information at www.talktofrank.com including how and where to access further support.

Paladin National Stalking Advocacy Service: 020 3866 4107.

Refuge: www.refuge.org.uk. Phone the 24-hour Domestic Abuse Helpline on 0808 2000 247 or visit www.nationaldahelpline.org.uk to access live chat (Monday to Friday 3–10pm).

Respect Men's Advice Line: 0808 801 0327.

Reading List

Briere, J. & Scott, C. (2006). *Principles of Trauma Therapy: A Guide to Symptoms, Evaluation, and Treatment.* London: Sage.

Cohen, J.A., Mannarino, A.P. & Deblinger, E. (eds) (2012). *Trauma-Focused CBT for Children and Adolescents: Treatment Applications.* London: The Guilford Press.

Dana, D. (2018). *The Polyvagal Theory in Therapy: Engaging the Rhythm of Regulation.* New York, NY: W.W. Norton.

Dana, D. (2020). *Polyvagal Exercises for Safety and Connection: 50 Client Centered Practices.* New York, NY: W.W. Norton.

DDP Network. *All about Dyadic Developmental Psychotherapy (DDP).* https://ddpnetwork.org/parents-carers/young-people.

Dursun, P. & Söylemez, I. (2020). 'Post-traumatic growth: A comprehensive evaluation of the recently revised model.' *Turkish Journal of Psychiatry, 31* (1), 59–69. doi:10.5080/u23694.

Fraus, K., Dominick, W., Walenski, A. & Taku, K. (2021). 'The impact of multiple stressful life events on post-traumatic growth in adolescence.' *Psychological Trauma: Theory, Research, Practice, and Policy.* Advance online publication. doi:10.1037/tra0001181.

Gordon, B.R., McDowell, C.P., Lyons, M. & Herring, M.P. (2017). 'The effects of resistance exercise training on anxiety: A meta-analysis and meta-regression analysis of randomized controlled trials.' *Sports Medicine, 47,* 2521–2532. doi:10.1007/s40279-017-0769-0.

Lee, D. (2012). *A Compassionate Mind Approach to Recovering from Trauma using Compassion Focused Therapy.* London: Constable and Robinson.

Perry, B.D. & Winfrey, O. (2021). *What Happened to You? Conversations on Trauma, Resilience, and Healing.* London: Bluebird Books.

Rothschild, B. (2010). *8 Keys to Safe Trauma Recovery: Take-Charge Strategies to Empower Your Healing.* New York, NY: W.W. Norton.

Rothschild, B. (2017). *The Body Remembers (Volume 2): Revolutionizing Trauma Treatment.* New York, NY: W.W. Norton.

Saxe, G., Ellis, B.H. & Kaplow, J.B. (2007). *Collaborative Treatment of Trauma-tised Children and Teens: The Trauma Systems Therapy Approach.* London: The Guilford Press.

Sissay, L. (2019). *My Name is Why: A Memoir.* London: Canongate Books.

Spence, J. (2021). *Trauma Informed Yoga: A Toolbox for Therapists.* Eau Claire, WI: PESI Publishing.

Sun-Reid, H. (2021). *Deep Sea Diving: Exploring the Process of Therapy within the DDP Model.* https://ddpnetwork.org/library/deep-sea-diving.

Ullrich Barcus, C. (2012). 'Hollies get prickly for a reason.' National Geographic. www.nationalgeographic.com/science/article/121220-holly-leaves-prickly-plants-science.

About the Authors

Bridie and Sue are clinical psychologists from CMCAFS (www.CMCAFS.com) who work with children, young people and those who care for them.

Reggie and Jade are young people with lived experience.

Index